Teilhard de Chardin
ALBUM

Preface by André George

Designed and edited by Jeanne Mortier and Marie-Louise Aboux

from the publications and letters of

Pierre Teilhard de Chardin, and from papers preserved at

the Fondation Teilhard de Chardin

Harper & Row, Publishers
New York and Evanston

We wish to record our deep gratitude to Claude Cuénot, to whose untiring researches we owe much valuable material; to the Directors of the National Museum; to Père Teilhard's family, and to his friends

FIRST EDITION

LIBRARY OF CONGRESS CATALOG
CARD NUMBER: 67-11289

Printed in France and Great Britain

Pilgrim of the Future

No preface could capture with more sympathy the spirit of this book than the words that follow, written by André George for the tenth anniversary of Père Teilhard's death; for the photographs collected here, which picture to us a life that has departed, and the accompanying sayings of a man who was so inspired by a passion for the discovery of the truth, bring out the continuity that ran through the life and work and thought of Pierre Teilhard de Chardin, and at the same time illuminate the spiritual adventure on which he himself embarked and which gave him so deep an understanding of the spiritual adventure of all mankind.

Ten years ago Pierre Teilhard de Chardin was an exile in New York; and there, on April 10th, a final heart attack ended his life. As a Jesuit, he had never faltered in his loyalty to the Society, and, far from home, he had maintained until the very end the silence imposed by the order to refrain from publishing his work.

We know from the man himself how much he suffered, for, the year before, he had written in his private notebook a saying of Bernanos: 'Every spiritual adventure is a Calvary'. Although he made no comment on the quotation, the words themselves are a sufficient indication of what he felt.

If we compare that sad date of 10 April 1955 with the present moment we find a very moving contrast. The tenth was Easter Sunday, and it indeed marked a resurrection. In contrast with what so often happens, the true birthday of the work coincides with the death of its author. Throwing off the semi-secrecy of mimeographed sheets limited to a few dozen copies, the whole body of his writings was now to come out into the open and to be published for all to read. In ten years no system of thought has come to be more widely known or has made more deep an impression on its age.

When, however, we speak of his work, what exactly do we mean? There are first of all his scientific writings. It was on these that his fame as a geologist and palaeontologist was founded, and it was these that led to his election to the Académie des Sciences. Apart from particular discoveries in the field of the vertebrates, we are indebted to him for an original approach to and a new way of studying the appearance of man and determining his place in nature—the 'phenomenon of man': and it is not long since our greatest living palaeontologist, M. Jean Piveteau, in a short but valuable book on Teilhard the scientist, made it clear how great is the debt we owe him.

On the other hand there is the whole of his posthumously published work in which is contained his thought; and the general public, who have no special interest in his purely technical writings, has discovered with enthusiastic delight this philosophical extension of his work, even though numbers of pure scientists are not too ready to follow Père Teilhard in this direction and are inclined to consider this body of work as lying outside the domain of science.

For the author himself, however, there was no division between what had been scientifically demonstrated and his vision of what the future held for mankind. Nobody was more one person than Teilhard. Just as he so combined the mystical life and scientific research that they became indissolubly one to a degree never before attained, so he set out to make his science help to mould our concept of the future. A powerful stimulus to men's minds and a great integrator of ideas, he spoke of himself as 'a pilgrim of the future'; and he had a deep-rooted urge to see everything pressing on, to try to build up a man who would be not a 'superman' but a 'fuller man', in the belief that evolution has hardly begun and that it cannot be other than spiritual. His priestly character expressed itself not in any religiosity but in a contagious ardour, and yet few religious have helped so many souls in the hidden places of their hearts. No man ever loved science more whole-heartedly, and none ever made his faith more a part of his life. No one has ever had more confidence in man and the world, and no one has orientated them more directly towards God.

He was as conscious as any of us of the tragedy that threatens the world, but he was always the man who looked both ahead of man and above man. He has often been called an optimist, but his optimism was a victory over pessimism. Some have thought to detect in him a sympathy with Marxism. The most convincing answer to this charge is contained in the words of Mr Senghor, the President of Senegal, 'Teilhard's thought has enabled us to dispense with Marxism and leave that stage behind'.

Pierre Teilhard de Chardin did not unlock every secret nor provide the solution to every problem. But few minds of such stature appear in this great era when so many things are dying, and so many more new things are being born: an era that so sadly needs a word of hope.

ANDRÉ GEORGE

Coat of arms of the Teilhard de Chardin family. The motto is from Virgil (Aeneid 6, 730): 'Fiery is their vigour, and of heaven their source'

Terra Mater

18 MAY 1875, EMMANUEL TEILHARD DE CHARDIN MARRIED BERTHE-ADÈLE DE DOMPIERRE D'HORNOY

ELEVEN CHILDREN WERE BORN TO THEM: ALBÉRIC, MARIELLE, FRANÇOISE, PIERRE, MARGUERITE-MARIE, GABRIEL, OLIVIER, JOSEPH, LOUISE, GONZAGUE, VICTOR

Berthe-Adèle de Dompierre d'Hornoy in 1875

Berthe-Adèle came from an ancient family in Picardy. She was a great-niece of Voltaire, and a grand-daughter of Jules Fiévet, 'the Saint of Lille'. Deeply pious, it was she who heard the children's catechism and taught them to read

A spark had to fall upon me, to make the fire blaze out. And, without any doubt, it was through my mother that it came to me, sprung from the stream of Christian mysticism, to light up and kindle my childish soul. It was through that spark that 'My universe', still but *half*-personalised, was to become amorised, and so achieve its full centration. ('*Le Coeur de la Matière*', 1950)

8

My Uncle Emmanuel, with his great height, fine bearing, bright eyes and cavalry moustache, used to terrify us, and his own children too, I think, in his spells of taciturnity. When he did speak, it was in unexpected bursts of pungent but kindly humour. He had been trained at the École des Chartes, and devoted his life to a patient study of the archives of Montferrand. . . . At the same time, as a real 'gentleman-farmer' he was personally running several estates. . . . A humanist with a strong cultural bent, he was a wide reader, particularly in history: he was a sound director of his children's reading, too, superintending their Latin lessons himself until they were ready for secondary school. Another of his contributions to the formation of their minds was to inculcate in them an interest in natural objects, and to encourage them to make natural history collections: insects, birds, stones. (*Marguerite Teillard-Chambon, writing under the name of Claude Aragonnès*)

Emmanuel Teilhard de Chardin in 1875

Bookplate of Emmanuel Teilhard de Chardin

The Church of Orcines, the parish church of the Teilhard family. In the background, the Puy de Dôme

1 MAY 1881: BIRTH AT SARCENAT OF MARIE-
JOSEPH-PIERRE, FOURTH OF THE TEILHARD
DE CHARDIN CHILDREN

The Château of Sarcenat

*View from a window at
Sarcenat. On the right, the
plateau of Gergovia; on the left,
Clermont-Ferrand*

The Château of Murol, belonging to the Teilhard de Chardin family

THE FAMILY SPENT THE SUMMER AT MUROL AND SARCENAT, AND THE WINTER AT CLERMONT-FERRAND

Fontfreyde, in Clermont-Ferrand, the town house of their Teillard-Chambon cousins

As far as I can go back in my childhood, nothing seems to me more characteristic or familiar in my inner disposition than the taste or irresistible need for some 'one and only sufficing and necessary' thing: in order to be fully at ease, to be completely happy, the knowledge that 'some essential thing' does really exist, to which everything else is no more than an accessory or, maybe, an embellishment. To know that, and unceasingly to rejoice in the consciousness of its existence. . . . ('*Le Coeur de la Matière*', 1950)

Pierre Teilhard de Chardin about 1884: detail from a pastel at Sarcenat

Emmanuel Teilhard de Chardin's children, about 1891. Sitting: Pierre, Françoise, Joseph, Gabriel. Standing: Olivier, Albéric, Marguerite-Marie

FAMILY LIFE WAS OFTEN ENLIVENED BY VISITS FROM THEIR COUSINS, THE TEILLARD-CHAMBONS

'My earliest memory? A little boy—he might have been three or four years old—at a children's fancy dress party that my parents gave in our house in Clermont, an old seventeenth-century mansion.

'These old houses, with their cellar-like entrances, their huge staircases, cold and damp, and their sombre, lofty, rooms, were a grim setting for our childhood. But they never stopped us from playing—the "terrible quartet" of boys, Albéric, Pierre, Gabriel and Joseph, wild and noisy, the girls more sedate, Françoise, Bernadette, two

Maries, two Marguerites. . . . We used to meet again, after vespers in the Carmelite Church. . . . From time to time we would think our room was going to be invaded: a great banging on the door and an unintelligible war-cry would frighten us out of our lives. Something awful and mysterious was going to happen. If, as sometimes happened, the gang caught one of us by surprise, plaits were pulled and there would be tears. However, the arrival of a nice *goûter* with jam and oranges soon restored peace.' (*Claude Aragonnès*)

Cirice Teillard-Chambon's children, about 1893. From left to right: Jeanne, Marcel, Alice, Robert, Marguerite

Volcanic chain (seen from the Puy de Dôme) which, from his earliest years, Pierre dreamed of exploring

Among the pleasures of that age (I can remember this very clearly) I was only really happy *in terms of* a certain fundamental joy. This consisted, generally speaking, in the possession (or the idea) of some object more precious, more rare, more consistent, more incorruptible . . .

I feel that with me every effort, even directed towards natural objectives, has always been a religious effort and substantially unique. I am aware of having been striving, in everything I have done, towards the Absolute. With any other objective, I do not think I would have found the courage for action. ('*Mon Univers*', *14 April 1918.* '*Écrits du temps de la guerre*')

The Jesuit school of Notre-Dame de Mongré, where Pierre Teilhard de Chardin was a boarder from 1892 to 1897

Pierre Teilhard at about the age of twelve

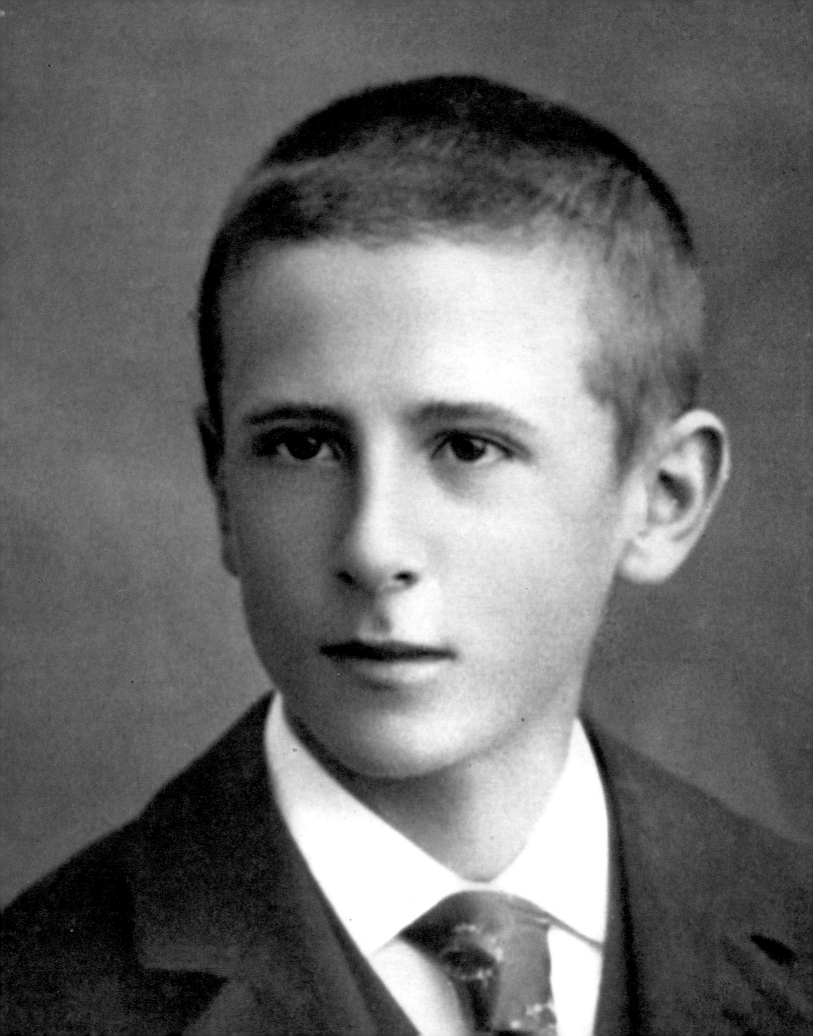

AT THE AGE OF ELEVEN, PETER WENT TO THE JESUIT SCHOOL OF MONGRÉ, IN VILLEFRANCHE-SUR-SAÔNE

Even if my passion for stones, and even more for antiquities, has not completely flared up again, I shall rekindle it during the summer holidays, for the fire is still in me, more active than ever. (*To his parents, 10 July 1892*)

WHEN IN THE FIFTH FORM, PIERRE TEILHARD WAS TAUGHT BY HENRI BREMOND

'Thirty years ago one of my classical pupils was a little fellow from Auvergne, very intelligent, first in every subject, but disconcertingly well-behaved . . . and it was only long afterwards that I learnt the secret of his seeming indifference. Transporting his mind far away from us was another, a jealous and absorbing passion—stones.' (*Henri Bremond, 'La Charme d'Athènes'*)

In the courtyard of the old family house in Clermont-Ferrand. From left to right: Pierre, Gabriel, Olivier

The philosophy class at the College of Mongré, in 1897. Pierre Teilhard is at the extreme right of the second row

PIERRE'S RELIGIOUS AWARENESS AND INTEREST IN SCIENCE GREW HAND IN HAND

There's no doubt about it, philosophy is certainly dry, but it's interesting; I'm afraid however, that I may be a bit tired of it before the year's finished ... I wish Guiguite would send me a little red retreat-notebook that's in the desk in the yellow room, and also a little prayer that's in her prayers of St. Gertrude. . . . I'm now first assistant in the Sodality. (*To his parents, 11 October 1896*)

Pierre at the age of 16

AT SIXTEEN, PIERRE TEILHARD FELT THAT HE HAD A VOCATION TO THE RELIGIOUS LIFE AS A JESUIT

'You will perhaps be surprised at not having heard from me sooner. The reason is that before writing to you I wanted to have another word with Père Desribes. I must tell you first of all that nothing is completely decided. At the same time (and those I've consulted agree with me) it does seem to me as though God is offering me a vocation to leave the world. You can well imagine that once I'm certain that I'm not mistaken, I shall answer the call; and I know, too, that you will be the last to raise any difficulties. All I now need is for our Lord to make me feel unmistakably what he wants of me and to give me the generosity of spirit that is needed.' (*To his parents, 4 June 1897*)

ON 20 MARCH 1899, PIERRE TEILHARD ENTERED THE JESUIT NOVITIATE IN AIX-EN-PROVENCE. LATER, HE WAS TO COMMENT, 'IT WAS A DESIRE FOR THE MOST PERFECT THAT DETERMINED MY VOCATION AS A JESUIT'

Old gateway to the Royal Bourbon College, which served as the Jesuit novitiate in Aix-en-Provence

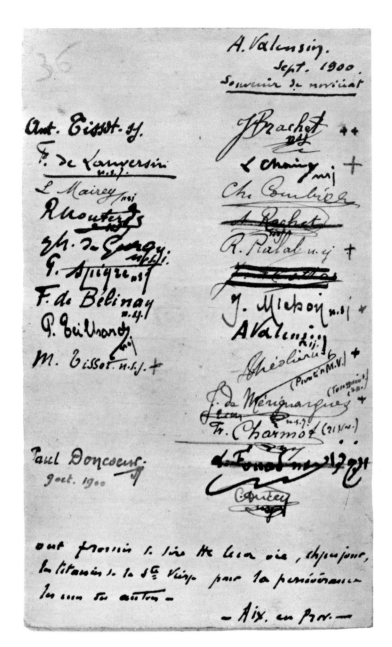

*Dedication to the Blessed
Virgin at the novitiate in Aix-
en-Provence, September 1900*

PIERRE TEILHARD'S TRAINING, AS WITH ALL JESUITS, WAS TO LAST
THIRTEEN YEARS: AS A NOVICE, A JUNIOR, A SCHOLASTIC, TEACHING
IN A JESUIT SCHOOL, STUDYING THEOLOGY, AND TERTIANSHIP

Thirty days' retreat, based on the Spiritual Exercises of
St. Ignatius, is the novice's first initiation into the life he will
be leading. This will include in turn:

— Two years as a novice, leading up to the taking of
simple vows.

— Two years of humane studies or 'juniorate', normally
leading to the *licence-ès-lettres*.

— Three years of scholastic philosophy and science.

— Two or three years teaching.

— Four years of theology, preparatory to ordination.

— Finally, one year as a tertian, culminating in the
taking of solemn vows.

'At the novitiate, he was a model novice, modest and apparently shy, but always ready to oblige others. . . . He was simple and unassuming, anxious not to appear in any way different from others, gay and lively, and a great walker. . . . A big fellow, very friendly and affable, with a ready smile, unobtrusive, well set up on his long legs, firmly planted on big feet, which were very turned out as he walked (an "atavistic" mark, he used to say, of the mountain folk). . . . A big fellow, very much the "gentleman", jolly and an agreeable companion, a lover of nature and fond of long walks, and, of course, most "edifying" as a novice.' (*Quoted from several sources by L. Barjon in his unpublished biography*)

ON 25 MARCH 1901, PIERRE TEILHARD DE CHARDIN TOOK HIS FIRST VOWS, AT LAVAL

'At last I'm a Jesuit: I haven't time to write much today but I want you to know just how happy I am that at last I belong entirely, through the Blessed Virgin, to the Sacred Heart. If only you knew the joy I feel now that I have at last given myself completely and for ever to the Society, particularly at a time when it is being persecuted. I prayed a great deal for all of you today, and I am sure that our Lord will never forget all you have done to assist my vocation. But you must always pray for me too, so that I can measure up to what God asks of me.' (*To his parents, 25 March 1901*)

*Saint-Michel, the Jesuit house in
Laval where Pierre Teilhard spent
his first year as a junior*

Bon-Secours, Jersey, where Pierre Teilhard de Chardin spent his second year as a junior

'As a junior in Jersey, I seriously considered the possibility of completely giving up petrology, in which I was then passionately interested, and devoting myself entirely to what are called "supernatural" activities. And, if I did not take completely the wrong road at that time, I owe it to the robust good sense of Père Troussard, the novice-master. In fact, all that Père Troussard actually did was to assure me that the God of the Cross looked as much for the "natural" development of my being as for its sanctification—without explaining to me how or why. But it was enough to enable me to see things in their proper perspective.' (*'Le Coeur de la Matière'*, *1950*)

1901. AS A RESULT OF LEGISLATION IN FRANCE DIRECTED AGAINST THE RELIGIOUS ORDERS, THE JESUITS WITHDREW TO THE CHANNEL ISLANDS, TO WHICH, DURING THE SUMMER OF 1901, THEY TRANSFERRED THEIR JUNIORATE

Pierre Teilhard, in Jersey, about 1902

1902–1905, WHILE PIERRE WAS A SCHOLASTIC IN JERSEY, WAS A PERIOD OF SUCCESSIVE TRIALS AT SARCENAT

Albéric Teilhard de Chardin, as a naval officer, about 1900

ON 27 SEPTEMBER 1902, ALBÉRIC, THE ELDEST OF THE CHILDREN, DIED AT SARCENAT

'If only you knew, my dear father and mother, how I am feeling that I love you more dearly at this moment. Albéric, too, loves and knows you better, and we must believe that he is looking after our family better on high than anywhere else, and that our Lord, too, since he sends a greater trial, loves all the more. . . . It is to Albéric himself and to the Blessed Virgin, who knows what it is to lose a son, that I am praying, to give you strength and bring you consolation.' (*To his parents, September 1902*)

MARGUERITE-MARIE, HIS YOUNGER SISTER, BECAME SERIOUSLY ILL WITH PLEURISY

Marguerite-Marie Teilhard de Chardin in 1900. Permanently bedridden, she became first the inspiration and later the President of the Catholic Union of the Sick

The Maison Saint-Louis in Jersey, where Père Teilhard did his three years as a scholastic, from 1902 to 1905

IN AUGUST 1904, HIS SISTER LOUISE DIED OF MENINGITIS, AT THE AGE OF TWELVE

'I am praying with all my soul to our Lord, to whom you so generously surrender your children, that he may soften your pain by making you feel that if he spares our family so little it is because he has found that it can serve him in a special way.' (*To his parents, August 1904*)

*The Jesuit philosophy students
from Lyons, in Jersey, 1905.
Pierre Teilhard is in the middle
behind the pot of flowers.
Auguste Valensin is standing in
the back row, second from the left*

SUMMER, 1905. PIERRE TEILHARD DE CHARDIN FINISHED HIS SCHOLASTICATE IN JERSEY

Auguste Valensin

Père Teilhard

'Among the novices was Père Auguste Valensin who later, when he was studying philosophy and theology, was to become, and remain until his death, a specially close friend.'

'Pierre Teilhard de Chardin, who in October 1902 embarked on his philosophical studies, was to spend all his leisure and holidays in scientific excursions around the island.' (*Louis Barjon, unpublished biography*)

In the middle of my preoccupations and secret joys, then—between the ages of ten and thirty years—I maintained and developed my contact with the cosmic 'in the solid state'. But already all around, in a half-subordinate way, there was the dawning attraction of the nature of plants and animals; and, underlying everything, one day (towards the end of the period) there came my initiation into the less tangible (but how exciting!) grandeur brought to light by the researches of physics. On both sides I saw matter, life and energy: the three pillars on which my inner vision and happiness rested. ('*Le Coeur de la Matière*', 1950)

IN SEPTEMBER 1905, PIERRE TEILHARD DE CHARDIN WAS SENT TO TEACH PHYSICS AND
CHEMISTRY IN THE JESUIT COLLEGE OF THE HOLY FAMILY, CAIRO, WHERE HE DID HIS THREE
YEARS' TEACHING

I haven't done much walking yet. In the first place, it's hot; and then, I'm not simply a passing visitor here, and I shall have plenty of time to enjoy Cairo in the winter. I have to think about my class too, and tidy up the physics room and laboratory, which need it badly. Later, I'll send you in one of my letters a sort of plan of Cairo. (*To his parents, 5 September 1905*)

General view of Cairo, map with notes by Père Teilhard for his family

I'm not without hopes of being able to send you one day a photograph of myself and of all the philosophy class. Talking of them, I must tell you that they've done very well: 11 passed out of 15, including 5 out of 6 in science. The lists of marks aren't out yet, but the average is more than satisfactory. (*To his parents, 31 May 1906*)

Last Sunday, I had to take charge of the choir-boys' holiday, which consists in taking them for a picnic and bathe at Matarieh, 'make the bathe' as they say in their French. (*To his parents, 25 June 1907*)

Jesuit fathers on a river-bank with a group of children. Père Teilhard is on the right

The natural history museum in the Jesuit College, Cairo

THE YOUNG TEACHER DEVOTES ALL HIS HOLIDAYS TO RESEARCH

A M. Priem in Paris, to whom I've sent all my harvests of fish-teeth, has told me that he is giving a note about them to the Geological Society of France. They include a new species and three new varieties, one of them 'Teilhardi!' (*To his parents, 6 December 1907*)

Fossilised fishes' teeth, found by Père Teilhard in Egypt (enlarged four times)

Here are my latest finds. M. Priem has talked at the Geological Society of France about my fishes' teeth from Mount Mokattam and on the jaw-bone of the Sirenian. At New Year I spent a week in Upper Egypt and I brought back from the Minya deposits a store of echinids which are the delight of M. Fourtau. He is writing an article about them ... these results show what one can do in between classroom duties and the various school chores, if you take the trouble to find a companion who doesn't mind spending the only free day in the week turning over stones right out in the desert, or detaching some big fossil from a rocky wall, in heat like a furnace. (*To a religious, 12 March 1908*)

The East flowed over me in a first wave of exoticism. I gazed at it and
drank it in eagerly—the country itself, not its peoples or its history
(which as yet held no interest for me), but its light, its vegetation, its
fauna, its deserts. . . . ('*Le Coeur de la Matière*', *1950*)

The Pyramids of Giza

SOME YEARS LATER, MEMORIES OF EGYPT WERE TO STIMULATE THE WRITING OF 'LA VIE COSMIQUE'

'*The world is still being created*, and in the world *it is Christ who is being fulfilled*.' When I had heard and understood this saying, I looked, and I saw, as though in an ecstasy, that through all nature I was immersed in God. ('*La Vie Cosmique*', *1916*)

Plate xi, illustrating Professor A. C. Seward's article in the Quarterly Journal of the Geological Society of London, 69, 1913. The relevant figures are 7 and 9

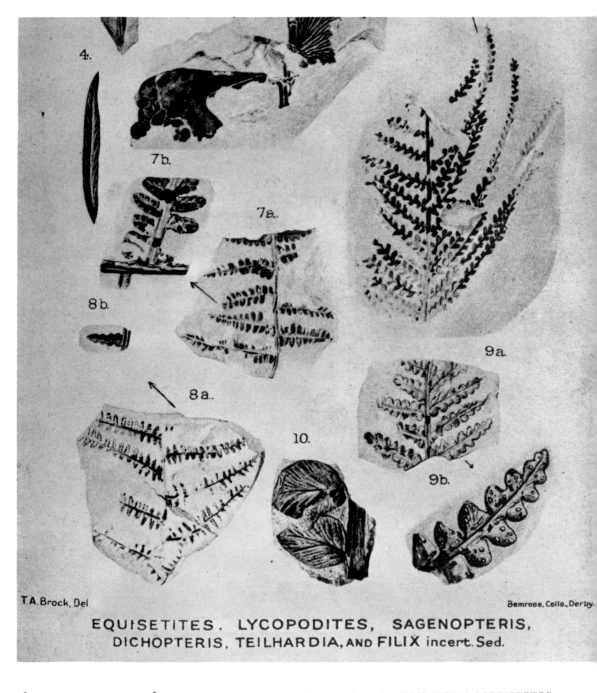

EQUISETITES, LYCOPODITES, SAGENOPTERIS, DICHOPTERIS, TEILHARDIA, AND FILIX incert. Sed.

WITH HIS FRIEND PÈRE PELLETIER, PÈRE TEILHARD WAS CONSTANTLY BUSY WITH SCIENTIFIC EXCURSIONS

Speaking of geology, the description of my fossil plants (from Hastings) has come out in the journal of the Geological Society of London. Among others, there's a genus Teilhardia and a species Teilhardi. Palaeobotany holds the record for oddly-named genera: at any rate, it's a mark of great kindness on the part of Professor Seward, who wrote the paper. (*To his parents, 16 May 1913*)

Père Teilhard de Chardin, Hastings, 1911

DURING THIS PERIOD, PÈRE TEILHARD BEGAN TO SEE THE UNIVERSE IN ITS ONENESS

All that I can remember from that time (apart from the magic word 'evolution' that continually came back to my mind like a refrain, like something desired, like a promise, like a summons . . .)—all I can remember is the extraordinary solidity and intensity I saw in the English countryside about that time—at sunset in particular—when the Sussex woods seemed to be charged with all the 'fossil' life that I was then looking for, from cliffs to quarries, and in the clays of the Weald. Sometimes it really seemed to me as though suddenly some sort of universal being was about to take on shape in nature before my very eyes. ('*Le Coeur de la Matière*', *1950*)

IN 1911, TWO MONTHS BEFORE PÈRE TEILHARD'S ORDINATION, HIS SISTER FRANÇOISE, SUPERIOR OF THE CONVENT OF THE LITTLE SISTERS OF THE POOR IN SHANGHAI, DIED OF SMALLPOX, AT THE AGE OF THIRTY-TWO

Françoise Teilhard de Chardin, about 1910

'Heart of Jesus, give me a heart that is filled with ardour and generosity, that thrills with joy when sacrifices have to be made; a heart whose zeal knows neither fatigue nor obstacle; a heart whose only love in your heart, and whose only knowledge is your name.' (*Prayer of Françoise Teilhard de Chardin*)

Our greatest consolation, surely, is that it is difficult to imagine a holier or more beautiful end. Françoise had, indeed, found just the death she wished for above all: in China and for China. Our Lord is giving her her reward before its time has come: we have no right, even, to regret the good she would have done had her life been longer. The fine life is the life that fulfils God's plans. (*To his parents, 7 June 1911*)

24 AUGUST 1911. PIERRE TEILHARD DE CHARDIN IS ORDAINED PRIEST, IN THE PRESENCE OF HIS PARENTS

Photograph taken in England at Père Teilhard's ordination. From left to right, Pierre, Gonzague, Joseph, M. Teilhard de Chardin, Victor, Mme. Teilhard de Chardin

ORE PLACE (Hastings)

Ore Place, Hastings, where
Père Teilhard studied theology
from 1908 to 1912, and was
ordained priest

If you judge me worthy, Lord God, I would show to those whose lives are dull and drab the limitless horizons opening out to humble and hidden efforts; for these efforts, if pure in intention, can add to the extension of the incarnate Word a further element—an element known to Christ's heart and gathered up into his immortality.

I shall remind those who are successful and happy that their success involves something infinitely more lofty than the satisfaction of their own petty personality. They can and indeed must take delight—but in Christ, whose plentitude calls for a certain fulfilment in nature. And I shall teach them to discern, even in their joy, side by side with the selfishness that retires into itself and the sensuality that gloats, a *force* of well-being and personal development that can be used for the activity of their soul in God.

And above all, I shall tell those who suffer and mourn that the most direct way of using our lives is to allow God, when it pleases him so to do, to grow within us, and, through death, to replace us by himself. (*'Le Prêtre', 8 July 1918*)

Père Teilhard de Chardin, 1912

Marcellin Boule

IN 1912, PIERRE TEILHARD ATTENDED A COURSE IN THE LABORATORY OF MARCELLIN BOULE,
PROFESSOR OF PALAEONTOLOGY AT THE MUSEUM. BOULE ASSIGNED HIM A STUDY OF THE PHOS-
PHORITES OF LE QUERCY

My work is still going well. The only thing is that I am reaching the time
when my population of carnivores suggests more ideas to me than I can
manage to put in order. It's good practice. What is really rather pleasant
is to have a front seat and so get the benefit of having first choice. The
other day, the admirable M. Boule took me to admire in his drawer an
insectivore preserved in a piece of diorite (similar in appearance and age
to those from the Limagne (Oligocene), every hair of which you can see!)
(*To his parents, 27 November 1912*)

*Phosphorites from Le Quercy,
in the Natural History
Museum, Paris*

*The palaeontology section of the
Natural History Museum,
Paris*

At the Castillo cave. From left to right: Nels C. Nelson, Paul Wernert, Hugo Obermaier, Miles C. Burkitt, Pierre Teilhard de Chardin

JUNE 13
EXCAVATIONS IN
THE SANTANDER
AREA, IN SPAIN

What I've really been doing is to shift a great deal of earth and of stones, or watch them being shifted. In the morning, about 8 o'clock, that is, we go up to the cave, in our outlandish rig-out, and stay there till six in the evening, in the open air and wonderful sunshine, with a magnificent view in front of us. We haven't made any sensational find; (. . .) but even so I find it extremely interesting, since this is the finest collection of Quaternary dwelling places known at present. (*To his parents, 16 June 1913*)

At the Pasiega cave. Front left to right: M. C. Burkitt, Hugo Obermaier, an unidentified companion, Nels C. Nelson, Paul Wernert; in front, Père Teilhard

Pierre Teilhard de Chardin at the Castillo cave

I can assure you that seeing these traces of a mankind earlier than any known civilisation really gave us something to think about; it's wonderful to stand in front of it, alone, in an absolute silence that is broken only by the sound of water dripping from the stalactites. (*To his parents, 16 June 1913*)

At the Altamira cave. From left to right: Nels C. Nelson, the guide, Pierre Teilhard de Chardin

At the Pasiega cave. From left to right: Pierre Teilhard de Chardin, the Abbé Breuil, Nels C. Nelson

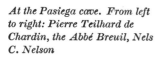

Fundamentally, I'm glad to have been at Ypres. I hope I shall have emerged more of a man and more of a priest. And more than ever I believe that life is beautiful, in the grimmest circumstances—when you can see God, ever-present, in them. (*To Claude Aragonnès, 28 May 1915*)

Claude Aragonnès (Marguerite Teillard-Chambon), Père Teilhard's cousin and close friend (1915). The war saw the beginning of their correspondence

I think one could show that the front isn't simply the firing-line, the exposed area corroded by the conflict of nations, but the 'front of the wave' carrying the world of man towards its new destiny. When you look at it during the night, lit up by flares, after a day of more than usual activity, you seem to feel that you're at the final boundary between what has already been achieved and what is struggling to emerge. (*To Claude Aragonnès, 23 September 1917*)

Morning coffee, on arriving in the trenches, Verdun, 1916. Père Teilhard is on the right

On the preceding page: Barbed wire entanglements in the sand-dunes

Douaumont fort, Verdun

24 OCTOBER 1916. THE VILLAGE OF DOUAUMONT IS TAKEN BY TEILHARD DE CHARDIN'S REGIMENT

In a few days' time we shall be thrown into battle for the recapture of Douaumont: a grandiose, almost a fantastic exploit which will mark and symbolise a definitive advance of the world in the liberation of souls. And I tell you this: I shall go into this engagement in a religious spirit, with all my soul, borne on by a single great impetus in which I am unable to distinguish where human emotions end and adoration begins. . . . And if I am destined not to return from those heights I would like my body to remain there, moulded into the clay of the fortifications, like a living cement thrown by God into the stone-work of the New City. (*Nant-le-Grand, 14 October 1916 ('The Pyx', in 'Christ in the World of Matter')*

Death surrenders us totally to God; it makes us enter into him; we must, in return, surrender ourselves to death with absolute love and self-abandonment, since, when death comes, all we can do is to give ourselves completely to the domination and guidance of God. (*To Claude Aragonnès, 13 November 1916*)

And so I started to think again, and to jot down in an exercise-book some notes about a subject that has always been for me the real problem of my interior life—rather as the question of Rome was for Newman or the meaning of the demands of the soul for Psichari: in my own case, it is how to reconcile progress and detachment, a passionate and legitimate love of the earth's highest development and the exclusive quest for the kingdom of heaven. How can one be as much a Christian as no other man, and yet more a man than anyone? (*To Père Fontoynont, 15 March 1916*)

WHEN THE MEDICAL OFFICER OF HIS UNIT, DR. SALZES, SUGGESTED THAT HE SHOULD ACCEPT THE POST OF CHAPLAIN, WITH THE RANK OF CAPTAIN, STRETCHER-BEARER TEILHARD ANSWERED: 'I AM OF MORE USE IN THE RANKS; I CAN DO MORE GOOD THERE. DO ME THE KINDNESS OF LEAVING ME WITH THE MEN

The Troyon ravine in 1917.
Père Teilhard de Chardin is
above, on the right

Père Teilhard de Chardin in 1918

29th August 1915. *Mentioned in Divisional Orders.* 'Volunteered to leave the aid-post in order to serve in the front-line trenches. Displayed the greatest self-sacrifice and contempt for danger.'

17th September 1916. *Mentioned in Army Orders.* 'A model of bravery, self-sacrifice, and coolness. From the 15th to the 19th August he directed the teams of stretcher-bearers over ground torn by shell-fire and swept by machine-guns. On the 18th August he went out to within 20 yards of the enemy lines to retrieve the body of a fallen officer and brought it back to the trenches.'

20th June 1917. *Médaille Militaire.* 'A first-rate N.C.O. His sterling character has won him confidence and respect. On 20th May 1917 he deliberately entered a trench under heavy bombardment to bring back a casualty.'

21st May 1921. *At the request of his old regiment he was made Chevalier of the Légion d'Honneur.* 'An outstanding stretcher-bearer, who during four years of active service, was in every battle and engagement the regiment took part in, applying to remain in the ranks in order that he might be with the men, whose dangers and hardships he constantly shared.'

At Sarcenat, 1917. Behind M.
and Mme. Teilhard de Chardin,
from left to right: Pierre,
Gabriel, Xavier le Maréchal,
Olivier

Mme. Teilhard de Chardin, in 1914

IN 1914 PÈRE TEILHARD'S BROTHER GONZAGUE WAS KILLED; IN MAY 1918, OLIVIER DIED OF WOUNDS

For us, indeed, that is the end of one of the best parts of our family life: but we have instead something so infinitely precious! After all, was it not your dearest wish that your sons should serve and that their lives should 'amount to something'—much more than that they should grow old? You see, there are lives that you could not bear to see bent or become shut in or constricted, and yet you cannot see how they could just continue to grow. It was like that, I think, with Olivier. (*To his parents, 16 May 1918*)

ON 26 MAY 1918, AT SAINTE-FOY-LÈS-LYON, PÈRE TEILHARD MADE HIS SOLEMN VOWS

As far as I can, *because I am a priest,* I would henceforth be the first to become aware of what the world loves, pursues, suffers, I would be the first to seek, to sympathise, to toil; the first in self-fulfilment, the first in self-denial. For the sake of the world I would be more widely human in my sympathies and more nobly terrestrial in my ambitions than any of the world's servants.

On the one hand I want to plunge into the midst of created things and, mingling with them, seize hold upon and disengage from them all that they contain of life eternal, down to the very last fragment, so that nothing may be lost; and on the other hand I want, by practising the counsels of perfection, to salvage through their self-denials all the heavenly fire imprisoned within the three-fold concupiscence of the flesh, of avarice, of pride: in other words to hallow, through chastity, poverty and obedience, the power enclosed in love, in gold, in independence. ('*Le Prêtre*', *8 July 1918, in The Hymn of the Universe*)

SUMMER 1919. PÈRE TEILHARD WAS STAYING IN JERSEY, WHERE HE WROTE 'THE SPIRITUAL POWER OF MATTER'

Blessed be you, harsh matter, barren soil, stubborn rock: you who would yield only to violence, you who force us to work if we would eat.

Blessed be you, perilous matter, violent sea, untameable passion: you who unless we fetter you will devour us.

Blessed be you, mighty matter, irresistible march of evolution, reality ever new-born; you who, by constantly shattering our mental categories, force us to go ever further and further in our pursuit of the truth.

Blessed be you, universal matter, immeasureable time, boundless ether, triple abyss of stars and atoms and generations: you who by overflowing and dissolving our narrow standard of measurement reveal to us the dimensions of God. ('*The Spiritual Power of Matter*', *Jersey, 8 August 1919*)

22 May 1920, geological expedition to la Fère (Aisne). From left to right: L. Joleaud, Père Teilhard, J. Cottereau

At Whitsun (when you missed me) I was on an expedition in the Laon area. From the town I recognised perfectly la Malmaison and the ravine of the Garenne above Chavignon, where poor Chevan fell. And, to get to Terguier, I went through Ribécourt and saw the woods of Laigne and Carlepont. I find it hard not to regret those days: in any case, as you go over that ground again you feel a bit sad and ironic at having no one with whom to share such memories. (*To Dr. Salzes, 20 June 1920*)

IN THE CERTAINTY OF SERVING HIS FAITH THROUGH SCIENCE, TEILHARD'S PASSION FOR
RESEARCH CONTINUED TO GROW

Gradually (though we cannot yet say exactly in what terms, but without
the sacrifice of a single one of the facts, whether revealed or definitely
proved) agreement will be reached, quite naturally, between science and
dogma in the burning field of human origins. In the meantime, let us take
care not to reject the least ray of light from any side. Faith has need of
all the truth. (*'Fossil Men'*, *March 1921*, in *'The Appearance of Man'*)

*Pierre Teilhard de Chardin and
Paul Jodot at the gravel-pits of
Chelles (Seine-et-Marne),
13 March 1921*

22 MARCH 1922. TEILHARD WAS SUCCESSFUL AT THE ORAL EXAMINATION ON HIS THESIS ON THE MAMMALS OF THE LOWER EOCENE IN FRANCE

The oral examination amply confirmed the excellent impression produced by reading the manuscript. The way in which the questions making up the second thesis were treated brought out the candidate's teaching ability and clarity of mind. He is certainly marked out for a fine future in science. The board of examiners had no hesitation in conferring on him the title of doctor, with distinction. (*Note by Prof. E. Haug*)

11 April 1921. Geological expedition to Mount Bouquet, at Seynes near Alès, under the direction of Pierre Termier

I dream of a new Saint Francis or a new Saint Ignatius, to come and give us the new type of Christian life (at once more involved in and more detached from the world) that we need. (*To Père Valensin, 21 June 1921*)

Père Teilhard de Chardin, about 1923

The horizon widens

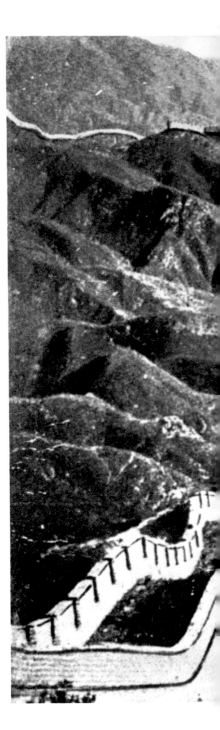

*Front of a post-card sent by
Père Teilhard to Alfred Lacroix,
shortly after his arrival
in Peking*

1923–1924. FIRST PERIOD IN CHINA

PÈRE TEILHARD WAS SENT BY THE MUSEUM TO TAKE PART IN A FRENCH PALAEONTOLOGICAL
MISSION DIRECTED BY PÈRE LICENT

I have landed up in a China more unsettled than ever, at the mercy, almost everywhere, of gangs of insurgent troops. The train I took from Nanking to here had been held up and robbed a fortnight before (and it's the biggest main-line train in China). In spite of these difficulties, I have good hopes of leaving, in a fortnight's time, for somewhere in Mongolia, when the preparations (more extensive than I imagined) for the expedition are complete. (*To the Abbé Breuil, 25 May 1923*)

The back of Père Teilhard's post-card to Alfred Lacroix shown on pages 6 6 - 7

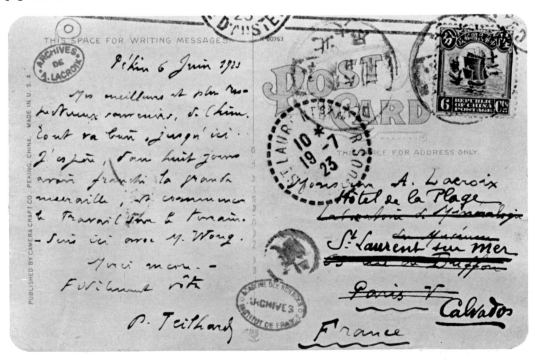

Map of Père Teilhard's journeys in China

Journey in 1923
Journey in 1924
Journey in 1926
Journey in 1927
Journey in 1929
Journey in 1930
Journey in 1931-1932 (Yellow Expedition)
Journey in 1932
Journey in 1934
Journey in 1935

Palaeolithic bed at Chou-Tan-Keou (Ordos)

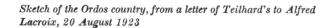
Sketch of the Ordos country, from a letter of Teilhard's to Alfred Lacroix, 20 August 1923

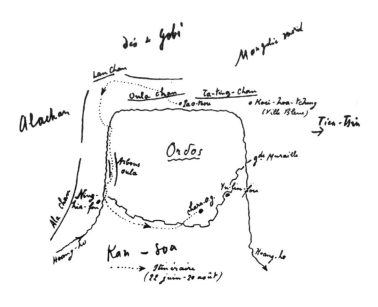

Three days ago, Licent and I found, sixty kilometres east of Ning-Hia-Fu, in the 'wall' of a torrent, a typical palaeolithic hearth, in perfectly stratified deposits (. . .) We are carrying on towards the Shara-Uso-Gol where last year Licent found his magnificent quaternary fauna and human femur. I hope now to understand these deposits properly, which almost certainly link up with those of the hearth we have just found (. . .) For the last two months we have never been able to go where we wanted to, and yet we have found something everywhere! The Lord, I do believe, is guiding us. (*To the Abbé Breuil, 25 July 1923*)

60-metre palaeolithic level, Shara-Uso-Gol (Ordos)

The Shara-Uso-Gol is a curious little river that winds in incredible meanderings at the bottom of a precipitous canyon 80 metres deep which it has dug out in the middle of a completely flat region of steppes and dunes. The walls of the canyon consist entirely of quaternary deposits. We did not do so well as Licent did last year (. . .) but even so we have a fine haul (fifteen cases already): masses of *Rhinoceros tichorhinus,* and gazelle; (. . .) and a base of a spiral antelope horn.

I've now arrived here, which is where I was making for, after a long detour—for we were obliged, because of the drought and the bandits, to go round on the northern side of the great loop of the Yellow River. I thought, when I came to China, that I wouldn't go far beyond the Great Wall, and now I know a big slice of western Mongolia. I don't regret these six weeks of wandering on mule-back through mountains and deserts. Not only has there been no lack of the picturesque but we have made, as we went along, some important geological and palaeontological finds which we were not expecting, and they are probably more valuable than all the bones of rhinoceros and horses and various other animals that we are now extracting from the cliffs of the Shara-Uso-Gol. (*To Léontine Zanta, 7 August 1923*)

Spiral antelope-horn brought back from the Ordos by Père Teilhard: now in the Museum of Natural History, Paris

Rhyolithic escarpment (Habo Tou)
north of Linn-Si, running along the Mongolian
Plateau. Expedition to the Dalai-Nor, 1924

When I am travelling by mule, for days on end, I say to myself, as I used to do, the 'Mass on the World' that you know, and I believe I say it now with more clearness of mind and conviction even than before. (*To Léontine Zanta, 7 August 1923*)

Since once again, Lord—though this time not in the forests of the Aisne but in the steppes of Asia—I have neither bread, nor wine, nor altar, I will raise myself beyond these symbols, up to the pure majesty of the real itself; I, your priest, will make the whole earth my altar and on it will offer you all the labours and sufferings of the world.

One by one, Lord, I see and I love all those whom you have given me to sustain and charm my life. One by one also I number all those who make up that other beloved family which has gradually surrounded me, its unity fashioned out of the most disparate elements, with affinities of the heart, of scientific research and of thought. And again one by one—more vaguely it is true, yet all-inclusively—I call before me the whole vast anonymous army of living humanity; those who surround me and support me though I do not know them; those who come, and those who go; above all, those who in office, laboratory and factory, through their vision of truth or despite their error, truly believe in the progress of earthly reality and who today will take up again their impassioned pursuit of the light. (*'The Mass on the World', 1923*)

Erosion in the loess over the Red Earth, Manchuria

We geologists, who have come here to the Ordos in search of the Bad Lands, we shall not be seduced by the comfortable peace of the gently rolling fields. No, we shall make our way into the deepest clefts in the mountain, where the Red Earth stands out like wounded flesh under the thick layers of grey. (*September 1923*)

*Père Teilhard de Chardin on
an ancient bridge, on the
imperial highway near Sien-Hsien*

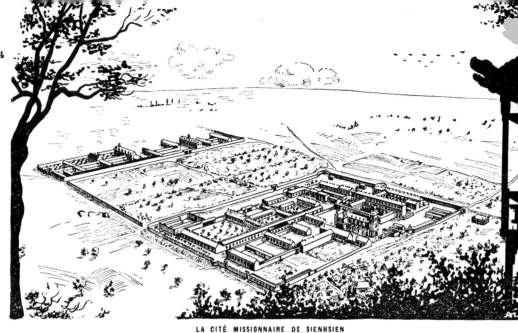

The mission city of Sien-Hsien

LA CITÉ MISSIONNAIRE DE SIENHSIEN

Couvents
des Auxiliatrices et du Précieux Sang.

Collège.
Séminaires.

Cathédrale.
Évêché.

Maison de Philosophie.
Noviciat.
Résidence.

I am just back from Sien-Hsien, from the depths, that is, of the Cheli mission. I am not sorry to have made the journey, for it has added considerably to my knowledge of the Chinese and their missionaries. . . . Sien-Hsien is a large fortified dwelling similar to the one I saw in Mongolia, but older and therefore bigger. It is quite a shock when you're inside its walls or stone ramparts to find, in the middle of a sea of cultivated fields, a little Christian city with a huge printing works, a college, a brewery, a mill, and nuns. From the outside you'd imagine you were coming to a Trappist monastery. (*To Claude Aragonnès, 10 February 1924*)

SEPTEMBER 1924. PÈRE TEILHARD RETURNED TO FRANCE AND TO TEACHING AT THE INSTITUT CATHOLIQUE AND GIVING TALKS TO STUDENTS AT THE SCHOOLS FOR ADVANCED STUDIES. FACED WITH THE NEED TO RECONCILE RECENT DISCOVERIES ABOUT THE ORIGIN OF MAN WITH THE DOCTRINE OF ORIGINAL SIN, HE WROTE A FEW PAGES ON THIS QUESTION FOR THE CONSIDERATION OF THEOLOGIANS. THE PAPERS FOUND THEIR WAY TO ROME—AND EXILE FOLLOWED.

It's done—I am being moved from Paris, and the most I can hope for is to be left here for another six months to finish my work on hand, and get ready for going back to China next Easter with my friend Licent. My dear friend, help me a little—I've been keeping up appearances, but, inside me, there's something like real agony, a real storm (. . .) It's essential that I should show by my example that even if my ideas appear an innovation, they still make me as faithful as any man to the old attitude. (*To Père Valensin, 16 May 1925*)

ON 10 JUNE 1926, PÈRE TEILHARD ARRIVED IN TIENTSIN, AND BEGAN TO WRITE 'LE MILIEU DIVIN'

I have settled down to the little book I plan. I want to write it slowly, quietly—living it and meditating on it like a prayer. (*To Claude Aragonnès, 7 November 1926*)

1926. VISIT TO PEKING OF ALFRED LACROIX, PERMANENT SECRETARY OF THE ACADÉMIE DES SCIENCES

Peking, January 1927. From left to right: M. and Mme. Lacroix, M. Bouillard, an engineer in Peking, Wong, Mme. Bloch, Père Teilhard

Père Teilhard de Chardin at the Institute of Higher Studies, Tientsin

For the last two weeks I have been practically all the time in the company of M. Lacroix, with whom are his wife and Madame B., sister-in-law of Sylvain Lévy, the director of the Franco-Japanese Centre at Tokyo. I was heartily delighted to meet my old friend and teacher again. He is one of the three or four finest examples of a man of science that I know. (*To Claude Aragonnès, 17 December 1926*)

Les Espas, home of the
Bégouën family, in the Ariège

PÈRE TEILHARD TOOK THE OPPORTUNITY OF SHORT VISITS TO FRANCE TO TAKE BACK TO THE
MUSEUM THE FRUIT OF HIS EXPEDITIONS

I arrived here in time to see Breuil for 48 hours and to receive some good
advice from him. Now, I am almost alone, in great peace, among the little
limestone hills, pitted with countless caves filled with a wealth of prehistoric life, looking across to the Pyrenees. Tall, bare, granite crests mark
the Spanish frontier, and before you come to them, foothills rounded and
wooded like the Bois du Roi. (*To Léontine Zanta, 1 September 1928*)

*Walking at Le Chambon,
with his cousins and
Léontine Zanata*

Let yourself be carried along by events, once they are too strong for you. You have a great influence on many minds you are in contact with. Do not worry if you find this form of activity somewhat sporadic or disconnected. It is not essential that we should completely and distinctly understand our life, for it to be good and worth-while. Often a life is fruitful through a side of it that one might be inclined to think little of. (*To Léontine Zanta, 20 May 1924*)

*Le Chambon, home of
the Teillard-Chambon
family, in Auvergne*

It was just by chance that I tried this visit to Somalia and Abyssinia, guided by the general principle of my life that one should lose no opportunity of trying out or finding out things: and it proved to be longer and more fruitful than I anticipated. (*To Père Valensin, 25 February 1929*)

HENRI DE MONFREID PLACED HIS DHOW AT THE DISPOSAL OF PÈRE TEILHARD

I examined the banks of living coral to my heart's delight: they're a real marvel. The water is crystal clear, and in it the red and green and streaked madrepores swell, cluster or spread out, and in the middle of this forest a whole world of bizarre fishes is moving around, red and yellow, black, blue, purple—glittering like humming-birds. But in spite of all these charms, I am in a hurry to get away to the Harar. (*To the Abbé Bréuil, 4 December 1928*)

In the gulf of Tadjoura, between Obok and Jibuti. On Père Teilhard's left, little Daniel de Monfreid

In the valley of the Tela, northwest of Obok. Père Teilhard is above, on the left

'So as not to scare the natives of these still extremely barbaric tribes, Père Teilhard wore a turban.' (*Related by Pierre Lamare*)

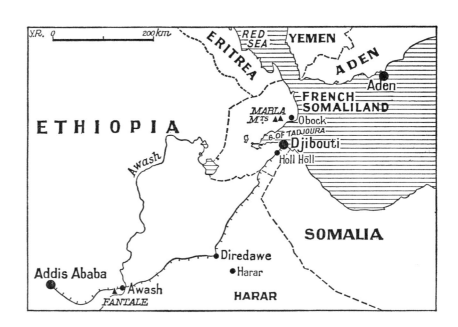

After we had ridden a couple of hours, the train crossed a small viaduct over a gloomy, romantic chasm, at the bottom of which ran a tiny river, and which presented, moreoever, a fine geological cross-section. As this tempting sight disappeared, my companion could not keep from crying out: 'Oh, if only they could stop the train here! Isn't it too bad that we can't get out and take a look at that!'

Well, hardly was the rash wish out of his mouth when Clank! Clank!—and the train jarred and jerked to a sudden stop. The locomotive had gone off the track . . . Teilhard and I profited by the resultant half-dozen hours of delay to examine the picturesque, shadow-filled gorge at our leisure. . . .

The train, once more or less set to rights, limped off, willing, but not able, to make up the lost time. It didn't get into Dire Dawa till about midnight. But the whole rest of the journey I spent in moderating Teilhard's wishful enthusiasms. 'Whatever you do, don't make any more wishes, because I don't know how you may stand with some of your superiors, but you certainly know the right people in heaven. If we're going to get any sleep before getting into Dire Dawa tonight, we don't want any more accidents, so please let's have no more petitions. We've had our miracle for the day.' (*Letter from Pierre Lamare to Claude Cuénot, August 1955*)

Père Teilhard de Chardin is on the right

Long low ridges, yellow in the winter drought; the winter here is the dry season. An implacable blue sky, and a north wind that can bring the night temperature down to 5° [Centigrade]. In front of me, a pretty lake covered with water-fowl, and surrounded by cattle. On the horizon a vast purple tabular chain, that must be at least 9,000 feet high. (*To Claude Aragonnès, from the Harar, Dire Dawa, 28 December 1928*)

The station at Holl-Holl on the railway from Dire Dawa to Addis Ababa: Père Teilhard de Chardin can be seen with his back to the camera

Cher Monsieur Lacroix,

J'espère que vous aurez bien reçu ma lettre 2 d'Obock vous donnant les explications concernant ma caisse n° 1, qui a dû partir de Djibouti ces jours-ci. J'ai donné des instructions à Marseille pour qu'on laisse suivre la caisse susdite au 61 rue de Buffon.

Cette fois-ci, je viens vous donner 921. détails sur mes observations et mes récoltes entre Diré-Daoua et Fantalé. (Entre Djibouti et Diré-Daoua je n'ai recueilli, aux environs de Hol-hol, qui me semblerait de rhyolite à liquophyses, rien de bien spécial à vous dire sur la région : massifs rhyolitiques émergeant de basaltes tabulaires). — La fig. 1 ci-jointe vous représente schématiquement la région parcourue. Je n'ai visité, en dehors du chemin de fer, que la région Fantalé - Jouenti, — et encore assez mal. Et tout en a raison, on prétend la région dangereuse dès qu'on s'éloigne à 500 mètres des stations. De plus, l'absence d'eau est complète dès qu'on quitte les stations. Il eût fallu une vraie expédition pour gagner le sommet du Fantalé. Ceci soit dit sans que vous m'excusiez si vous envoyez des renseignements beaucoup trop fragmentaires. — Chaque échantillon que je vous envoie a son étiquette explicative, dont le n° correspond aux chiffres des coupes (fig. 2 et 3), quand il y a lieu.

a) Volcan du Fantalé. — Cirque (600 m.?) au milieu d'une plaine parfaitement plane, revêtue d'une couche de brèche ignée rouge-clair, chargée de sidérium noir, présentant la curieuse propriété de ~~formes~~ des boursouflures disséminées (plus d'une centaine, sûrement) sur la plaine, comme de grandes taupinières. Chaque boursouflure est creuse, et la voûte tapissée de stalactites de lave, prouvant que la "bulle" s'est formée au moment de l'écoulement, et non sous l'influence des éruptions récentes (toutes voisines). Je n'ai pu voir si cette brèche à lave sous le Fantalé. Je croirais plutôt qu'elle en représente la dernière phase d'éruption (assez ancienne). — Je me suis monté qu'au 1/3 de la montagne. La base est formée de coulées foncées (analogues aux bancs 1 et 2 de l'Annexe, fig. 2), avec par-sant obsidienne. Mais, par des blocs isolés, je suppose qu'au-dessus (comme à l'Annexe) existe une série verte (Rhyolite-Pantellerite). Ce qui me fait admettre

4-5 m.
stalactite de lave
10 - 20 m.

Père Teilhard de Chardin with the Fantalle volcano in the background

AT THE FANTALLE VOLCANO

The Fantalle Volcano. It rises up (600 metres?) in the middle of a perfectly flat plain, covered with a layer of light green igneous breccia, overlaid with black obsidian, which has the curious property of forming blisters scattered over the plain (over a hundred of them, I'm sure), like huge mole-hills. Each blister is hollow and the roof is covered with lava stalactites, showing that the 'bubble' was formed while the lava was flowing and not as a result of recent eruptions (in the vicinity). (*To Alfred Lacroix, 14 December 1928*)

Looking towards the Fantalle volcano

On the next page: general view of the hill of Chou-Kou-Tien

ON 15 MARCH 1929 PÈRE TEILHARD DE CHARDIN WAS BACK IN TIENTSIN.
IMPORTANT EXCAVATIONS WERE BEING CARRIED OUT AT CHOU-KOU-TIEN IN THE WESTERN
HILLS

A letter from Ting urgently begged me to get down to Chou-Kou-Tien, 30 miles south of Peking, to study with two Chinese the geology of the site and supervise the organisation of the year's new excavations. To take charge of Chou-Kou-Tien was too important a job for me to think of refusing. So I started back for the capital with my camp-bed and some provisions. A little Ford took me and my two companions over impossibly bad roads to a village near the dig. Well, one way and another, I'm pretty satisfied. In the first place, from the technical point of view, I think I have been able to throw a little more light on the history of what will in future be a very celebrated site. (*To Claude Aragonnès, 6 May 1929*)

TELEGRAM (IN ENGLISH) FROM TEILHARD AND DAVIDSON BLACK TO MARCELLIN BOULE,
28 DECEMBER 1929:

'New Year Greetings. Recovered Chou-Kou-Tien uncrushed adult Sinanthropus skull entire except face. Letter follows.'

The Chou-Kou-Tien team in 1929. From left to right: Pei, Young, two students, Père Teilhard de Chardin, Davidson Black, George Barbour

Site 1 at Chou-Kou-Tien, where the first Sinanthropus skull was found

Since I came back to China a year ago, things, as you have perhaps suspected, have moved a great deal and changed for me. (...) There is continually more work, more possibilities, more results, more offers. And then there comes this Sinanthropus skull, which I did not, of course, discover myself, but which I was in the nick of time to deal with from the geological and palaeontological angle. Such coincidences 'madly' increase my faith in the presence of God in our lives. (*To the Abbé Gaudefroy, 7 February 1930*)

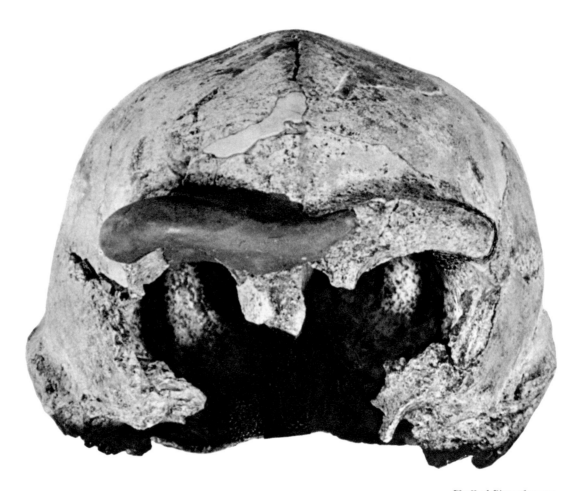

Skull of Sinanthropus

It is an extraordinary thing. For a century scientists have been examining with unheard of subtlety and daring the mysteries of the atoms of matter and of the living cell. They have weighed the electron and the stars. They have divided the plant and animal world into hundreds of thousands of species. They are trying, with infinite patience, to link the human form anatomically with that of the other vertebrates. Passing to a more direct study of our own zoological type, they are trying to analyse the driving forces in human psychology or to bring out the laws that govern the exchange of products and services in the increasing complexity of society. And yet, with all this work going on, hardly anyone has yet thought of asking the question that really matters: What precisely is the phenomenon of man? In other words, and more exactly, what place is held, and what purpose is fulfilled, in the observed development of the world, by the astonishing power of thought?' (*'The Phenomenon of Man', November 1930, in 'The Vision of the Past'*)

All discoveries, especially in palaeontology, owe something to chance. In the case of Sinanthropus, it should be noted, this chance has been reduced to a minimum. What started with a stroke of luck, method has patiently completed. The discovery of Sinanthropus is not, as some people have believed, the result of a happy stroke of the pick. It represents three years of systematic and devoted work. (*'Sinanthropus pekinensis', 20 July 1930,* in *'The Appearance of Man'*)

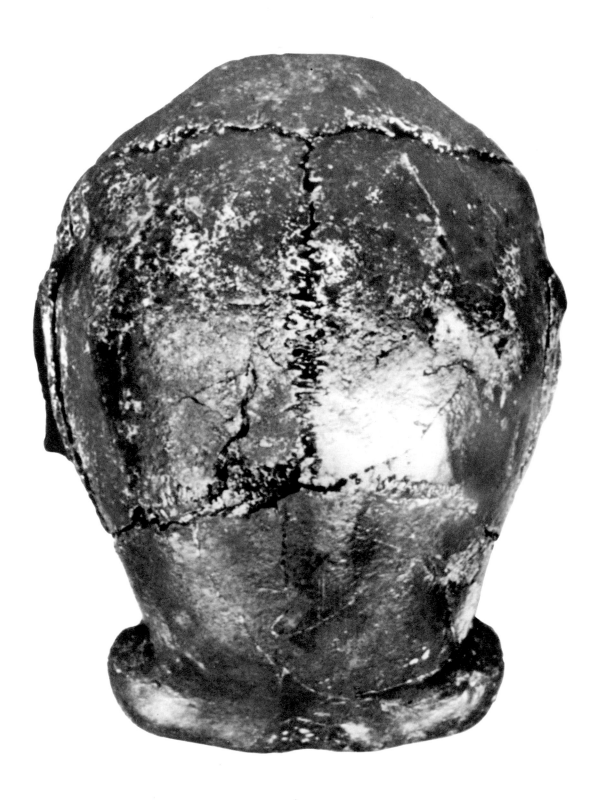

Wolf Camp

FROM JUNE TO JULY 1930 PÈRE TEILHARD DE CHARDIN TOOK PART IN THE AMERICAN CENTRAL ASIAN EXPEDITION, LED BY CHAPMAN ANDREWS. THE OBJECTIVES WERE KALGAN, AND THEN THE GOBI DESERT

Our blue tents are pitched at the edge of a fossil-bearing cliff, looking out over the immense flat surfaces of Mongolia: the terraced levels, uniformly grey with a tinge of delicate green, have a look of magic when the rays of the setting sun skim over them. There is nothing in sight but a few yourts beside the streams, and we work in absolute solitude, our only companions the wolves, eagles and gazelles, which last always provide the bulk of our diet, The same gaiety and family spirit prevails in the camp.

The work goes well. We have got hold of some authentic mastodon deposits—strange mastodons with an elongated jawbone rounded into a huge spoon. For my own part I am managing to link together satisfactorily the geologies of China and Mongolia (my principal objective) and I am vastly extending the horizons I include in my vision. (*To Claude Aragonnès, 29 June 1930*)

During the American Central Asian expedition, in Mongolia. In the foreground, on the left, Père Teilhard de Chardin; on the right, Professor W. Granger (?)

Père Teilhard de Chardin, 1930

Street in Peking, about 1930

I plan to leave Peking on 10th September, and to go back via Siberia, arriving in Paris on the 25th. . . . We will have a lot to talk about. I feel older, physically; but I feel that I 'see' things better than ever—so simply, so coldly and so passionately all at once! I will be able to tell you about my plans for my own inner development—for lack of any plans for outward radiation, where I am always pretty restricted. (*To Léontine Zanta, 22 August 1930*)

FROM SEPTEMBER 1930 TO THE END OF JANUARY 1931, PÈRE TEILHARD WAS FOR A SHORT TIME BACK IN PARIS

Père Teilhard de Chardin, Paris, 25 January 1931

Back in Peking, I had the pleasant surprise of examining a second Sinanthropus skull, found while I was away. This second specimen is not more complete than the first (or hardly so, in some points). Even so, it is still a fine one. Moreover, the identity of form in the two fossils is complete. I have indeed been lucky to be mixed up in this business. Such good fortune has the result of making me exclusively and madly enamoured of the Divine influence that guides the world. (*To Père de Lubac, 31 July 1930*)

Chou-Kou-Tien. Pocket (site 12)

Père Leroy and Père Licent on their visit to Chou-Kou-Tien

The fish-pocket (site 14)

Fissure filled with broken stones (site 4)

ON HIS RETURN TO PEKING, TEILHARD ASSESSED THE IMPORTANCE
OF WHAT HAD BEEN DISCOVERED

In brief, the more one observes the Choukoutien fissure, the more one is struck by the analogies between its deposits and those of the classical contents of European caves. But what makes the Chinese site exceptionally interesting is that stratigraphically and palaeontologically it appears to be considerably older than any of the caves that have hitherto furnished remains human in type in Europe. (*'The Sinanthropus of Peking', 1931, in The Appearance of Man*)

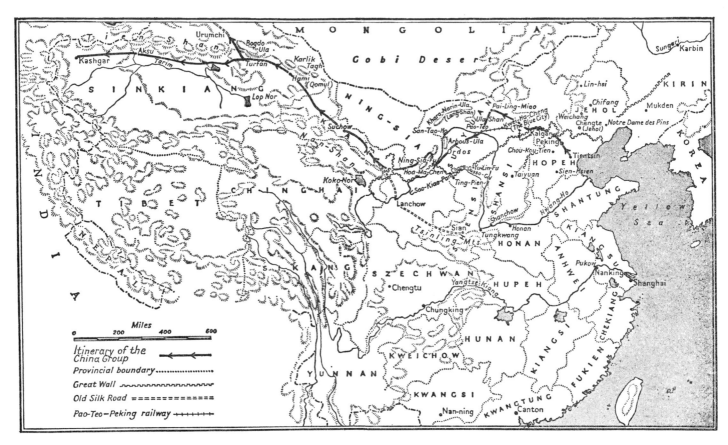

Since 1929, André Citroën and his factory-manager had been preparing an expedition into Central Asia. They hoped to rediscover the ancient 'silk road' and at the same time to demonstrate the qualities of the Citroën equipment.

The expedition was divided into two groups. The Pamir group, led by G.-M. Haardt, started from Beirut and crossed the Himalayas. The China group, led by Victor Point, started from Peking and crossed China by the Gobi Desert.

Route followed by the China group, including Père Teilhard

TEILHARD WAS NOW JUST FIFTY YEARS OF AGE. WHILE WAITING TO SET OUT, HE WROTE
'L'ESPRIT DE LA TERRE'

Père Teilhard de Chardin in 1931. Official Yellow Expedition photograph

With the support of what religion and science have been teaching me for the last fifty years, I have tried in this to make my way out into the open. I wanted to get clear of the fog and see things as they really are (...) And the first thing I saw was that only man can be of any use to man in reading the secret of the world. (*'L'Esprit de la Terre', 9 March 1931*)

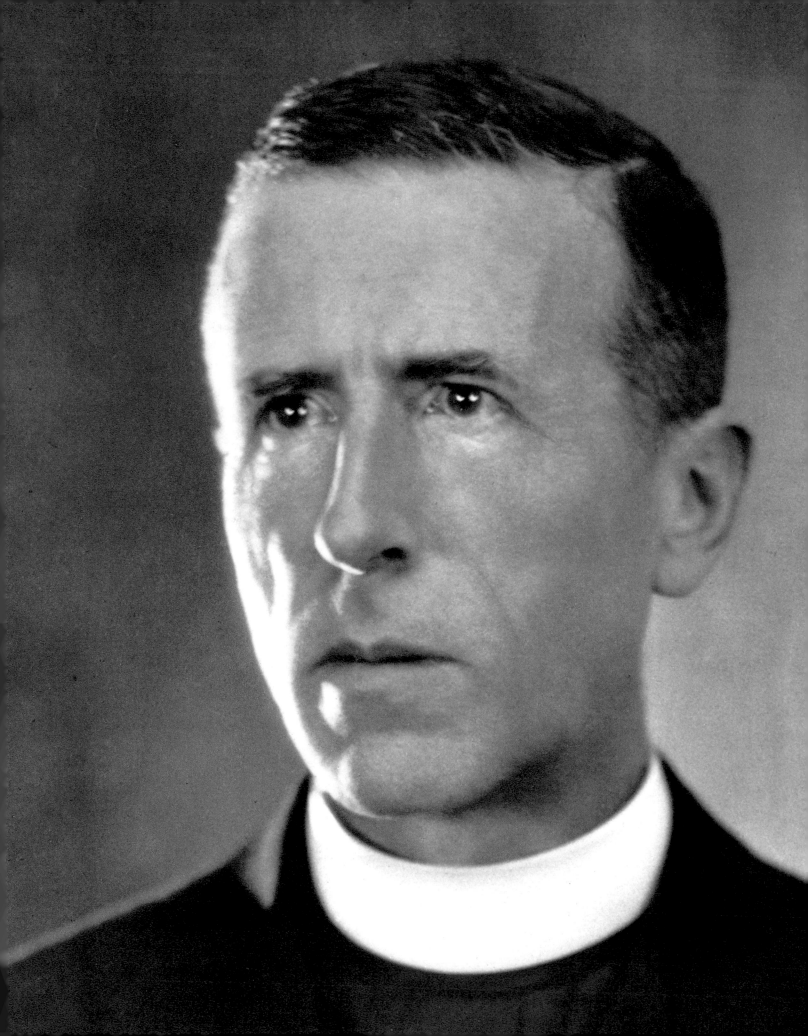

Truck stuck in sand dunes.
On the right, Père Teilhard in silhouette

THE START

I am going on ahead, to the west, with two supply trucks. (*To Claude Aragonnès, 4 May 1931*)

In Tientsin. The day before the start, Père Teilhard de Chardin with one of the expedition's vehicles

FIRST TROUBLES

'From Pei Ling Miao to Wuni Wusu, the convoy followed the tracks of the trucks in open and at first slightly undulating country; Père Teilhard, recognising some palaeozoic outcrops, regretted that we could not stop to hunt for fossils.' (*Georges Le Fèvre, 'La Croisière Jaune'*)

One evening, at Pei Ling Miao, in Mongolia (it was 25 May 1931)—while a slain kasarka, a golden duck, hung from the tent roof over their beds—Teilhard, upon hearing a doubt expressed about the existence of God, asserted, without changing his voice, and as if stating an algebraic theorem: 'God is a very simple choice, the choice between a Yes and a No, between a plus sign and a minus sign. This is a choice that none of us can escape.' (*Claude Cuénot, 'A Biographical Study'*)

Vehicles of the Citroën expedition in the Gobi desert

TWO METHODS OF FINDING THE WAY

We were travelling at the time across completely broken country, the vehicles following one another into deep, parallel ravines, with sides not very tall, but so narrow as to be practically tunnels. As night fell, Point saw his nine vehicles entering in turn a sort of trench. The head of the convoy had been halted at the top of a col that ended in a sheer drop. It was impossible to find a way out. The next day, at first light, we had to set about methodically to find a route (. . .).

Père Teilhard said that we could do so if we could find a granite 'dyke' furrowed by still very recent valleys. 'We'll never,' he said, 'get out if we follow the valley-bottoms. They'll all end in a sheer drop. But the ridges that divide the valleys are flat, and if we follow them we may be able to find a way out.'

Meanwhile, however, Goumbo (the guide) had already, bit by bit and casting about, worked out a sort of road that might be improved by pick and shovel. This track, carefully reconnoitred, ran in more or less the same direction as Teilhard's. We thought this a most remarkable coincidence and asked Goumbo how he had done it.

'I followed the tracks of the wild animals—when they go to drink they always look for the easiest route.' (*Georges Le Fèvre, 'La Croisière Jaune'*)

28 June 1931. The Battle of Khami.

'The unexpected arrival of the vehicles seemed to have been turned to good use by the Chinese, who were deployed as riflemen and holding the ridges. We could already see their red and yellow flags with regimental colours. As we came closer we found a tragic scene. The road was blocked with the corpses of men and animals. Terrified children were hiding under overturned carts. A woman was weeping and wailing by the side of a dying man, her husband. A Chinese soldier had emptied the pockets of one of his dead comrades and was hastily pulling off his shoes. Tethered camels were stumbling against their ropes. Some of them had shaken off their loads, which were lying on the ground. Tugging madly at their halters, they were tearing their nostrils, with piercing screams. The ground was littered with empty cartridge cases and ammunition pouches.

'Have you a doctor?'

But Delastre had already set up his little aid-post, and, with Père Teilhard, who volunteered to help, was immediately surrounded by some thirty casualties. The badly wounded were brought to him, but for these nothing could be done. They had lost too much blood. The lead bullets the Shantu use inflict terrible wounds, and death is generally from haemorrhage. (*Georges Le Fèvre, 'La Croisière Jaune'*)

Dr. Delastre, the expedition's doctor, and Père Teilhard, treating the wounded

In the bustle of camp life I am beginning to collect my thoughts and write a little. I am making a first rough draft of a memorandum on the results of my researches between Kalgan and Urumchi. I think, too, I shall in the end write a series of reflections under the title *Prière dans la durée*. It is to be at the same time an interpretation, a making one's own, an acceptance and a transfiguration of the world, put forward in the context of the deepest and most commonly shared of man's questionings, anxieties and emotions: those of discovering, undergoing, growing old and waiting—all of which are effects or forms of duration. (*To Claude Aragonnès, 28 August 1931*)

At the Urumchi camp. Lt.-Commander Point, Brull the engineer, and Père Teilhard de Chardin

ON ARRIVING, IN MID-JULY, AT URUMCHI, THE GROUP FOUND THEMSELVES PRISONERS

At Urumchi; Père Teilhard is on the right

Aksu, 8 October 1931. Front row, left to right, Audouin-Dubreuil, G.-M. Haardt, and Père Teilhard de Chardin, who had gone to meet them

Si Val, Cdt Pecqueur, M.O. Williams, Morizet, Le Fèvre, G.-M. Haardt, Penaud, Teilhard, Audouin-Dubreuil

8 OCTOBER 1931, MEETING AT AKSU OF THE CHINA AND PAMIR GROUPS

'A golden dust rises from the horses' hooves on a road spangled with blue shadows and bordered by a stream. By the stream, a fisherman in overalls, sleeves rolled up, drops his rod, waves his arms and runs up: "So you're all here at last! We've had a pretty long wait for you, you know!"

' "Father! My good friend, my dear friend!"

'Greetings and embraces: we all dismount and lead our horses by the bridle.' (*Georges Le Fèvre, 'La Croisière Jaune'*)

At Aksu. From left to right, G.-M. Haardt, Jacovleff, Audouin-Dubreuil, Père Teilhard de Chardin

107

IN OCTOBER 1931, A SMALLER TEAM WAS ALLOWED TO EXPLORE THE DEAD CITIES OF THE GOBI

The team consisted of Hackin, Père Teilhard, Williams, Jacovleff, Sauvage and his two operators, and immediately got down to work. Père Teilhard spent his ten days in a geological survey of the area, and the others, led by Hackin, concentrated, each in his own particular field, on a thorough study of the site and its remains. (*Georges Le Fèvre, 'La Croisière Jaune'*)

The Yellow Expedition's geologist

The Pleistocene terraces and caves at Bäzäklik:
Near these caves is the site of the ancient city,
half-buried in the sand, which provides one of the last
traces of Greco-Buddhistic civilisation on the edges of
the Gobi Desert

At the end of the Pliocene, immense and widespread erosion spread out sheets of gravel around the rocky massifs of the mountain chains, while clouds of lighter sediments were continually carried towards China by the winds. This began the massive process of denudation. Then, during the Quaternary, the hollows were still filled by great Nors of whitish, sterile mud, while the last dusty deposits of loess, swept up by the glacial winds, fell like snow on the mountains of Shansi, Shensi and Kansu. The desert was established once and for all.

This, put briefly, is the vision of the past which—like a mirage that rises, shimmers and becomes ever more substantial, sharper and clearer—is seen by a geologist crossing the Gobi. ('*La Croisière Jaune*', *report by Père Teilhard*)

Père Teilhard de Chardin at the
time of the Yellow Expedition

BETWEEN KHAMI AND SU-CHOW, DECEMBER 1931

'We were travelling then for twenty hours out of the twenty-four. And gradually our exhaustion grew harder to bear than the cold. Everyone succumbed to a dangerous inertia. Being forced to remain still, we were frozen, our curiosity was numbed and we sank into an extraordinary state of sluggishness (. . .) Twice a day, a quick meal was taken in the open. You had to hurry before the boiling soup served out by Gauffreteau in metal bowls (which was cold before you swallowed it), turned into an icy mush. We used to eat it greedily, standing up, and at night, silent, muffled up in furs that made movement almost impossible, indistinguishable one from another, we stood around the mess-truck like strange puppets with shadows distorted by the headlights (. . .)

Exhaustion was general. We piled in, standing, huddled up or squatting, into the one tent that we could manage to put up to shelter us from the squalls, with blue hands and miserable expressions, like those of wanderers lost in the depths of the desert. "Anyone want more noodles?" Gauffreteau would dismally ask.' (*Georges Le Fèvre, 'La Croisière Jaune'*)

In the frozen heart of Asia

Finishing up the noodles in the Gobi desert. Père Teilhard de Chardin is the first on the left

CONTINUING THE DESERT TRAIL

'Not much excitement in this Gobi!'

Raymond found it singularly lacking in character in the winter. 'How do you mean, lacking in character?' protested Père Teilhard. 'On the contrary, it's a particularly suitable field for surveying. Can't you see the ground is littered with prehistoric implements?'

His observant eye would spot the smallest worked stone that stood out, red, against the grey bareness of the wind-swept earth. He would have his vehicle stopped, get out, pick up a pebble and then another. Was this indeed a real cultural centre of the Middle Palaeolithic? No, it was, rather, the southern limit of an extremely ancient human wave that started from Siberia. At the same time, he realised that he was in the presence of a quartzite industry, Mousterian in appearance. (*Georges Le Fèvre, 'La Croisière Jaune'*)

Part of G.-M. Haardt's last letter to his wife (1 March 1932)

d'horreur naît le rayon de
lumière des Pères Missionnaires
qui, isolés de tout sur ces terres mau-
dites y vivant dans un renoncement
complet. C'est près de Liangchow chez
les Pères allemands de la Société du
Verbe Divin que nous avons passé
le premier jour de l'année. Ce matin là
le Père Teilhard de Chardin avait consen-
ti à dire une messe pour les membres
de l'Expédition. C'était un spectacle
bien émouvant de voir réunis, dans
cette petite chapelle perdue au cœur de
la Chine tous ces hommes dans leur
équipement de route se recueillant
devant Dieu avant d'affronter à nouveau
tout l'imprévisible qui les séparait encore
de leurs buts, à l'aurore de cette
année nouvelle..
Le Père Teilhard de Chardin est un
Prince de l'Église mais il a, autant
qu'il est possible de le posséder, l'esprit

'Some day I shall write, for your son, an account of this extraordinary journey across the most inaccessible parts of China, at a time when the most terrible chaos prevailed and there was no law but the law of the strongest. It is a mysterious country, forbidden to all Europeans. And yet one ray of light emerges from this vision of horror: it comes from the missionary fathers who, completely cut off in these accursed parts, live a life of absolute self-denial. We spent New Year's Day with the German brothers of the Society of the Divine Word. That morning Père Teilhard had agreed to say Mass for all the members of the expedition. It was a most moving sight to see them all together in that little chapel lost in the heart of China: there, in their travelling kit, they recollected themselves in the presence of God, before once again facing all the unforeseeable difficulties that still stood between them and their destination, as the New Year dawned.

'Père Teilhard de Chardin is a prince of the Church but he has the expeditionary spirit as fully as any man can have it.'

ON NEW YEAR'S DAY, 1932, PÈRE TEILHARD SAID MASS AT THE LIANG-CHOW MISSION, IN THE PRESENCE OF ALL THE MEMBERS OF THE EXPEDITION. AUDOUIN-DUBREUIL KEPT A COPY OF THE ADDRESS

My dear friends, we have met this morning, in this little church, in the heart of China, in order to come before God at the beginning of this new year. Of course, probably for not one of us here does God mean, or seem, the same thing as for any other of us. And yet, because we are all intelligent beings, not one of us can escape the feeling, or reflection, that above and beyond ourselves there exists some superior force, and that, since it is superior to ourselves, it must possess some superior form of our own intelligence and our own will.

It is in this mighty presence that we should recollect ourselves for a moment at the beginning of this new year. What we ask of that universal presence which envelops us all, is first to reunite us, as in a shared, living, centre with those whom we love, those who, so far away from us here, are themselves beginning this same new year.

Then, considering what must be the boundless power of this force, we beseech it to take a favourable hand for us and for our friends and families in the tangled and seemingly uncontrollable web of events that await us in the months ahead. So may success crown our enterprises. So may joy dwell in our hearts and all around us. So may what sorrow cannot be spared us be transfigured into a finer joy, the joy of knowing that we have occupied each his own station in the universe, and that, in that station, we have done as we ought.

Around us and in us, God, through his deep-reaching power, can bring all this about. And it is in order that he may indeed do so that, for all of you, I am about to offer him this Mass, the highest form of Christian prayer.

In the Gobi desert: investigating evidence of Pliocene tool-making

'Not far from the banks of the Yellow River, around the loop of which they are travelling, the nine vehicles have just come to a halt. It is dusk. Père Teilhard de Chardin, the geological specialist, is pointing out the silhouette, standing up from a recumbent fold in the Ordos, of a giant mass of rock, known, he says, as Genghis Khan's anvil.' (*'L'Illustration', July 1932*)

LATER, PÈRE TEILHARD PUBLISHED THE RESULTS OF THESE TEN MONTHS OF EXPLORATION

Climbing on to the caterpillars as though I were mounting a camel, I asked only one thing of the expedition: to take me across Asia (...). So far as that goes, I have had what I asked for. I often strained at the bit when I was unable to follow up the marvellous opportunities that presented themselves. But, as someone truly said, the drawbacks of a thing are part of the thing itself. In the end I had nearly doubled my store of information about Asia. For that, ten months of life, even at the age of fifty, is not too much to pay. (*To Claude Aragonnès, 21 December 1931*)

Emmanuel Teilhard de Chardin towards the end of his life

'My life has been made up of sorrows and disappointments. I have put my trust in God and now I can see that it has led up to a victory that I had never hoped for nor even dreamt of.' (*From the last page of Emmanuel Teilhard's notebook*)

JULY 1932–JULY 1933
EXPEDITION TO SHANSI; BRIEF VISIT TO FRANCE; BACK TO PEKING; DEPARTURE, AT THE END OF JUNE, FOR AMERICA

I am just back from the Washington Congress. I have found these three months in America profoundly interesting, especially the last four weeks, the whole of which I spent in Oregon and California (. . .). I wanted to see the Pacific coast, because I knew it must contain illuminating analogies with certain conditions you find in China (intrusion of mesozoic granites, pronounced end-of-Tertiary and Quaternary plication). I was quite overwhelmed: I found all I wanted, and more. (*To the Abbé Breuil, 10 September 1933*)

Père Teilhard playing with a chipmunk (a rodent unknown in Europe) near the Crater Lake, Oregon

ON HIS RETURN TO TIENTSIN, TEILHARD WAS WORRIED BY POLITICAL DEVELOPMENTS IN EUROPE

As for tangible realities, you—and everyone—must have been struck by some of the really extraordinary aspects of the human crisis today. Fascist doctrines strike me more and more (in so far as they are racialist and nationalist) as an abnormal reaction—sterile, retrograde and therefore temporary. (*To Père de Lubac, 9 December 1933*)

George Barbour, in New York, 1934

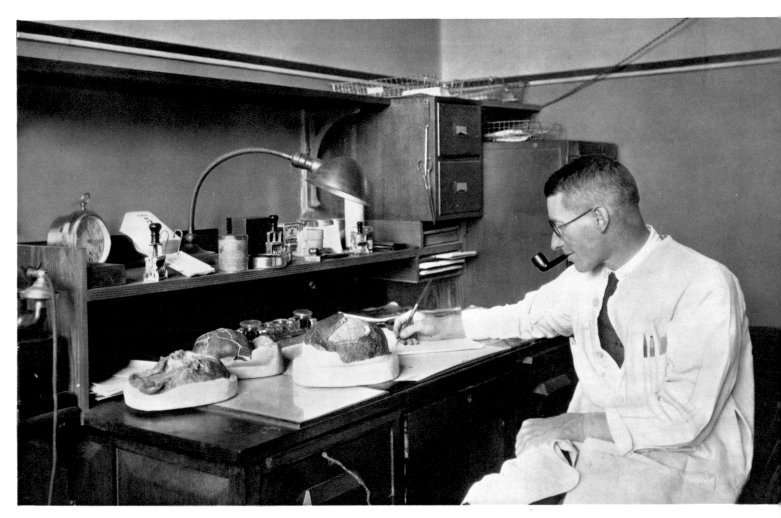

Davidson Black in his laboratory

16 MARCH 1934, SUDDEN DEATH OF DR. DAVIDSON BLACK, DIRECTOR OF THE GEOLOGICAL SURVEY AT PEKING

Davidson Black died suddenly in the evening of the day before yesterday (*heart failure*). His heart had been giving trouble for some time, and five weeks ago we had a warning of what might happen. We were hoping that he was pulling round, but then the end came suddenly. Black was feeling better (or seemed to be); he had just been talking briskly with some friends and was full of plans, as usual. A moment later he was found dead, by this table, in this Lab. you know so well, between Sinanthropus and the skull from the Upper Cave. (*To the Abbé Breuil, 18 March 1934*)

In the confusion following Black's death, and in the stifling atmosphere of 'agnostic' regrets that surrounded it, I swore to myself, on the body of my dead friend, to fight more vigorously than ever to give hope to man's work and search for truth. (*To Max Bégouën, 10 April 1934*)

From left to right. Young, (unidentified), Teilhard de Chardin, during their journey up the Yangtze-Kiang with George Barbour

MAY 1934. ASCENT OF THE YANGTZE-KIANG, WITH PROFESSOR BARBOUR, WONG, AND TWO CHINESE GEOLOGISTS

We arrived here yesterday, after a splendid journey through the gorges; they have certainly not been overrated, especially from the geologist's point of view. For more than 60 miles the powerful waters force their way between high walls of cliff with frequent rapids, where you can read almost the whole geological story of China. (*To Claude Aragonnès, Chungking, 30 May 1934*)

Père Teilhard de Chardin and the Abbé Breuil at Chou-Kou-Tien

Père Teilhard and the Abbé Breuil at the Ming tombs

The Suez Canal, about 1930

MAY TO SEPTEMBER 1935: BRIEF VISIT TO FRANCE
FROM THE SHIP IN WHICH PÈRE TEILHARD WAS TRAVELLING TO INDIA HE WROTE:

So here I am, back again to my vagabond existence. My enthusiasm has lost the freshness it had of old; but what I like to do is to follow my destiny and trust myself to it, though never, indeed, have I known less where it was leading me: probably to nothing but a new series of moves until I end my days by the roadside. (*To J. Teilhard de Chardin, 14 September 1935*)

The past has revealed to me how the future is built (...). Now that the fundamental discovery has been made, that we are carried along by an advancing wave of consciousness, does anything of importance remain to be disclosed in what has been left behind us? Certain rhythms or impulses, perhaps, that are still hidden from us by the slenderness of our knowledge at this actual moment. (*To Claude Aragonnès, 8 September 1935*)

To catalogue everything, test everything, understand everything. What is above, higher than the air we breathe; what is below, deeper than light can penetrate. What is lost in sidereal space, and what the elements conceal. . . . The sun is rising ahead. . . . The past is left behind. . . . The only task worthy of our efforts is to construct the future. (*'The Discovery of the Past', 15 September 1935, in 'The Vision of the Past'*)

Marguerite Teillard-Chambon (Claude Aragonnès)

Père Teilhard de Chardin in India, 1935

Père Teilhard helping to extricate a vehicle from the sand in the Salt Range

AUTUMN 1935. EXPEDITION TO INDIA WITH HELMUT DE TERRA

We left ten days ago, de Terra and I, and since then we have been wandering about the Salt Range, sometimes by camel, sometimes by car, sometimes under canvas, and sometimes (as today) in one of the comfortable bungalows that the British government has put up at frequent intervals for the convenience of travelling sahibs. (*To Claude Aragonnès, 16 October 1935*)

APART FROM HIS GEOLOGY, TEILHARD'S LIFE CONTINUED ON THE SPIRITUAL PLANE OF THE 'MILIEU DIVIN'

To begin with, in action I adhere to the creative power of God; I coincide with it; I become not only its instrument but its living extension. And as there is nothing more personal in a being than his will, I merge myself, in a sense, through my heart, with the very heart of God. ('*Le Milieu Divin*', November 1926–March 1927)

Teilhard in the Salt Range

In India, 1935

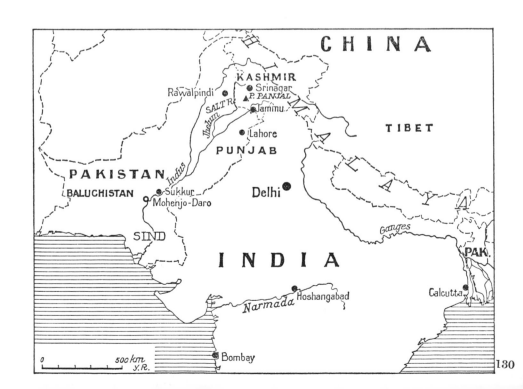

130

Helmut de Terra
photographing a child

It's picturesque country, but three-parts desert, cracked and stony. There are moments when I might be back in Egypt or Abyssinia. All the plants and trees are thorny. I am extremely well and surprised to find myself 'so young'. Every day we are on foot nearly all day long and I feel no tiredness at all. Not a cloud in the sky. (*To Claude Aragonnès, 16 October 1935*)

Père Teilhard with a group of local women

I am glad, once again, that I obeyed life's suggestions and made the 'act of faith' of coming to India. (*To Mme. Haardt, 29 October 1935*)

Père Teilhard de Chardin looking over the Narbada valley

Nucleus, lower valley of the Narbada

IN TEILHARD'S MEDITATIONS AT THIS TIME WERE ALREADY GERMINATING IDEAS WHICH HE
LATER EXPRESSED IN 'THE PHENOMENON OF MAN'

So let us bow our heads in tribute to the anxieties and joys of 'trying all and discovering all'. The passing wave that we can feel was not formed in ourselves. It comes to us from far away; it set out at the same time as the light from the first stars. It reaches us after creating everything on the way. The spirit of research and conquest is the permanent soul of evolution.

AT THE INVITATION OF PROFESSOR R. VON KOENIGSWALD, PÈRE TEILHARD DE CHARDIN
STOPPED IN JAVA

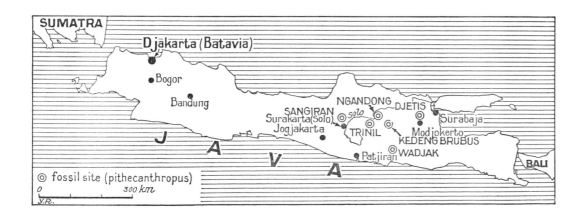

Every time I experience it again I become the more convinced that I was made for life in the tropics. I am intensely fond of the rich vegetation, the heavy vegetal scents, and even the thick clouds which after the daily downpour drift away from the mountain sides. (*To Joseph Teilhard, 21 January 1936*)

I have just spent four really *exciting* months in India and Java: masses of new stuff, good solid stuff, in the loveliest settings in the world. I have the feeling that I am building up something more and more extensive. Now I am hurrying back to Peking to see what effect the Japanese penetration is likely to have on conditions at the Geological Survey. (*To Père Valensin, 18 January 1936*)

Patjitan (Java): orang-utan site

I am as conscious as anyone of the gravity of the present situation for mankind (...) And yet some instinct, developed in contact with life's long past, tells me that for us salvation lies in the direction of the very danger that so terrifies us (...) We are like travellers caught up in a current, trying to make our way back: an impossible and a fatal course. Salvation for us lies ahead, beyond the rapids. We must not turn back—we need a strong hand on the tiller, and a good compass. (*'Esquisse d'un univers personnel', 4 May 1953*)

ON 7 FEBRUARY 1936, SHORTLY AFTER HIS RETURN, HE LEARNT OF THE DEATH OF HIS MOTHER

'My dear and saintly mother, to whom I owe all that is best in my soul.'

ON AUGUST 17TH, PÈRE TEILHARD'S SISTER MARGUERITE DIED

Marguerite Teilhard de Chardin towards the end of her life

'If we must succumb (...), let it be an active sacrifice, a renouncing of action in favour of a higher form of action. But, until the last sigh is drawn, we must keep ourselves alert for a task that is never finished. Then death will not be for us an end, or a desertion, but a happy homecoming to our Father's house.' (*'Le jour qui vient', Marguerite-Marie's last article*)

'O Marguerite my sister, while I, given soul and body to the positive forces of the universe, was wandering over continents and oceans, my whole being passionately taken up in watching the rise of all the earth's tints and shades, you lay motionless, stretched out on your bed of sickness: silently, deep within yourself, you were transforming into light the world's most grievous shadows.' (*Paris, 8 January 1950*)

Père Teilhard de Chardin, 1936

Meeting with Professor Grabau, Peking, 1936

(1) Wong Wen Hao, (2) Sven Hedin, (3) Professor Grabau, (4) Professor Horner van der Hedin, (5) Père Teilhard de Chardin, (6) P. H. Juan, (7) Dr. Günther Köhler, (8) Dr. Chaney, (9) Hilse Hanguer, (10) Dr. Ting

'*Truth* is simply the complete coherence of the universe in relation to every point contained within it. Why should we be suspicious of or underestimate this coherence just because we ourselves are the observers? We hear continually of some sort of anthropocentric illusion contrasted with some sort of objective reality. In fact, there is no such distinction. Man's truth is the truth of the universe for man: in other words it is simply truth.' ('*Esquisse d'un univers personnel*', *4 May 1936*)

Père Teilhard de Chardin, 1936

138

From the narrowly personal point of view, 1937 looks like being a laborious and complicated year, and my own life in general an unending pilgrimage. But I can see quite clearly that it would be a betrayal on my part not to take up my staff again and accept the routine of perpetual separations. (*To Joseph Teilhard de Chardin, 5 September 1936*)

Peking, February 1936. From left to right: Père Teilhard de Chardin, Lucile Swan, C. C. Young, Dr. Stevenson, Eddie Bien, Mrs. Stevenson, Olga Hinkel (?)

ON BOARD THE 'EMPRESS OF JAPAN', BOUND FOR THE U.S.A., PÈRE TEILHARD WROTE 'LE PHÉNOMÈNE SPIRITUEL'

The boldest of tomorrow's navigators will set out across the mysterious ocean of moral energies, which they will have to explore and humanise (. . .) What all of us, more or less, are lacking at present is a new formula to express what is meant by Holiness. ('*Le Phénomène Spirituel*', in the *Pacific, March 1937*)

Père Teilhard de Chardin, New York, April 1937

Philadelphia, 22nd March 1937. Fr. Edward V. Stanfort, of the Catholic College of Villanova, presents the Mendel medal to Père Teilhard de Chardin, in recognition of his work

18–23 MARCH 1937. PHILADELPHIA CONGRESS

At Philadelphia I am to meet, under the aegis of the Carnegie Institute, a group of people interested in the study of human origins. (The idea is to set up a systematic plan for investigations that may take me again next year to India and north of the Himalayas). There I shall meet again de Terra, von Koenigswald (Java), Miss Garrod (England). As usual, I shall be the only Frenchman. At the beginning of April I shall go on to New York. (*To Joseph Teilhard de Chardin, 12 March 1937*)

Discussions at the Philadelphia Congress. From left to right: Professor Oswald Menghin (Vienna), G. H. R. von Koenigswald (Java), V. Gordon Childe (Edinburgh), Père Teilhard de Chardin

IN AUGUST 1937, PÈRE TEILHARD SAILED FOR CHINA FROM MARSEILLE. DURING THE VOYAGE HE WROTE 'L'ÉNERGIE HUMAINE'

In truth, each of us is called upon to respond, by a pure and incommunicable harmonic, to the universal Note. When, through the progress of our hearts towards love of the whole, we feel stretching out above our various strivings and desires the exuberant simplicity of an impulse in which all the countless shades of passion and action mingle and rise up while remaining distinct, it is then that at the heart of the mass of human energy we each draw nearer to the fullness of our effective powers and our personality. (*'L'Energie Humaine', 6 August 1937*)

Peking is fairly empty, but a good nucleus of friends remains, Lucile Swan for a start. She has just been working with Weidenreich on the restoration of the face of Sinanthropus: we had nearly all the materials but they had not been fitted together in place. The reconstructed individual (a complete head including the mandible) is a female: we call her Nelly, and I don't doubt you'll see her before long. (*To Max Bégouën, 21 October 1937*)

In Lucile Swan's studio, with 'Nelly'.
From left to right: F. Weidenreich,
W. Bosshard, Höppeli, Lucile Swan

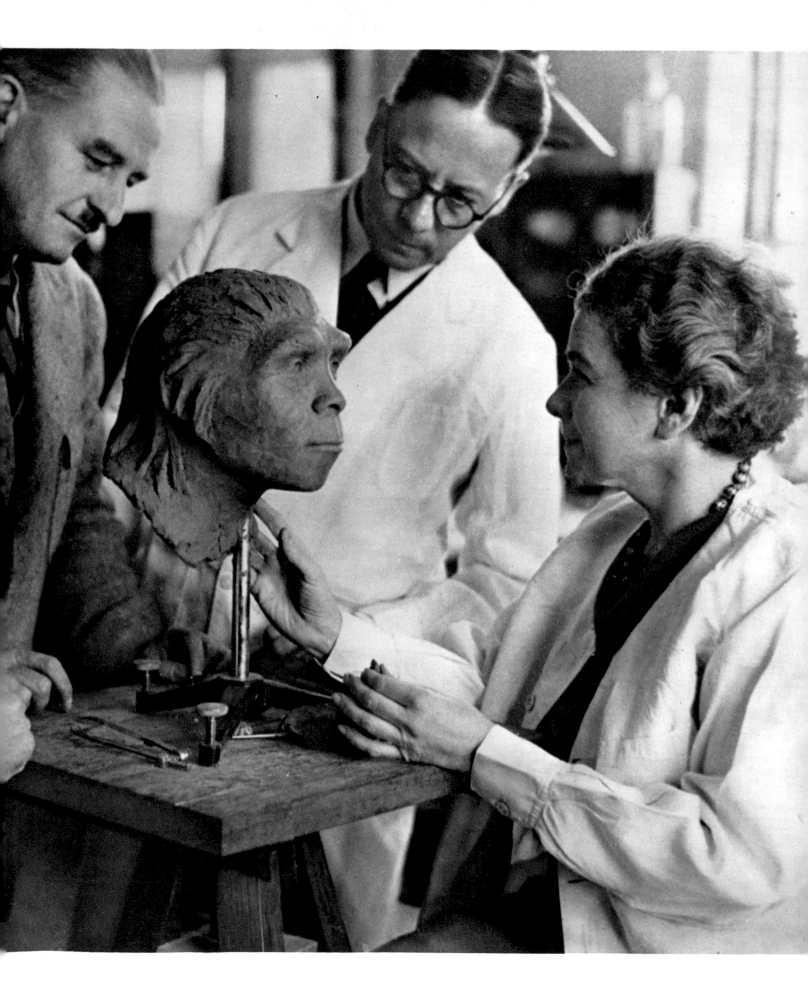

Encampment on the Shan plateau

BEGINNING OF 1938: BURMA EXPEDITION, WITH HELMUT DE TERRA

We left the Irrawaddy some days ago and are now working in the grandeur of the High Shan plateau: dense forests over which spring is scattering patches of cream, pink and flame—an odd country in which I don't know how many Shan tribes rub shoulders—including 'head-hunters'. (*To Max and Simone Bégouën, 28 February 1938*)

On the Shan plateau, Burma

IN THE IRRAWADDY VALLEY

On one of our evenings in the Irrawaddy valley, something unforgettable happened which illustrated Teilhard's generosity and friendship. Having made a long excursion up the valley in order to trace the development of certain geological formations, we returned to our camp at nightfall. I had blistered a foot during the lengthy tour, and had just removed my boots with a sigh of relief when I suddenly noticed that my notebook was missing. After a vain search, I was forced to conclude that I had left it at the site we had last examined (...). When I told Teilhard that I was going back to fetch my notebook with our Burmese guide he looked quite shocked and said he would go and look for it himself, since it was out of the question for me to walk about in the darkness with my sore foot.

Palaeolithic implements, Yenangyaung, Burma

The Irrawaddy valley, Burma

Deaf to my entreaties, he pulled on his tennis-shoes, called for the guide and vanished with him into the pitch-black night by the light of a pocket-lamp. When he returned some hours later and brought the notebook to my tent, his whole face was beaming with delight. (*Helmut de Terra, 'Memories of Teilhard de Chardin'*)

Palaeolithic gravel pits, Magwe, Burma

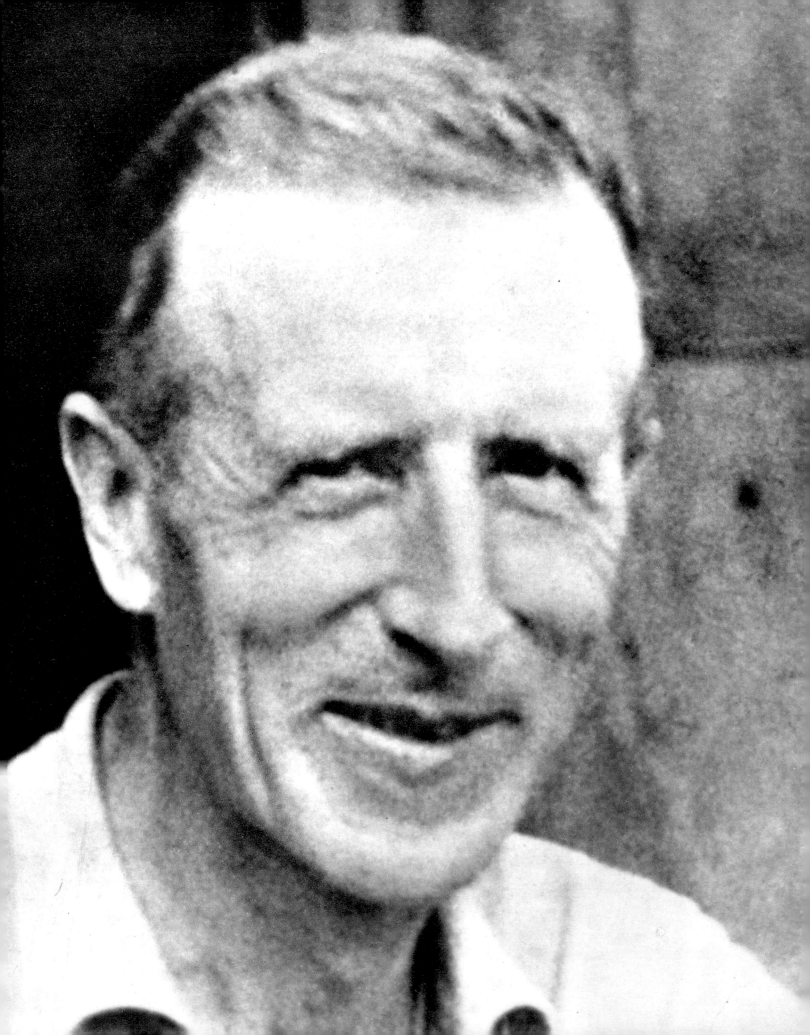

Père Teilhard de Chardin and Helmut de Terra, Java, 1938

RETURNING FROM BURMA IN MARCH 1938, TEILHARD DE CHARDIN PAID A SECOND VISIT TO JAVA

Pére Teilhard de Chardin,
Ralph von Koenigswald and
Helmut de Terra, in Java, 1938

Helmut de Terra and Père Teilhard, Java, 1938

Java is really an ideal country. I am just back from an expedition to an active volcano whose summit (crater) can be reached by car. The summit is covered with virgin forest, the lower slopes with tea and cinchona: luxury hotels along the road, bungalows with swimming pools. I prefer the real jungle—still, there's something very pleasant about this artificial beauty. (*To Joseph Teilhard de Chardin, 5 April 1938*)

Java, 1938
From left to right:
R. von Koenigswald, H. Movius,
Helmut de Terra, Teilhard

In the mud of the tropical forest, by the Solo river, Java

BY THE SOLO RIVER

Père Teilhard de Chardin and R. von Koenigswald at the Pithecanthropus monument to Dr. Eugene Dubois, Trinil, Java

Our march, which I shall never forget, took us along a narrow path in the hot and humid shade of huge bamboo thickets which occasionally afforded a glimpse of the river. Isolated bird-calls broke the stillness of the tropical forest. Knowing Teilhard's predilection for such sounds, I imagined that he must have been enjoying himself as he walked along ahead of me, but as soon as the path became swampy our mood of enjoyment vanished. Each step took us further into a black morass of glutinous, clayey mud which rose above our ankles. I saw Teilhard trudging ahead with bowed head. Like ours, his shirt was soaked with sweat and his khaki slacks encrusted with mud, but his tennis-shoes, which several times came off in the mud, proved an added hardship (. . .) Finally, at midday, we reached a small group of huts, where we sank exhausted on to a tree-stump and drank cool milk from some coconuts which the natives brought us from neighbouring palm-trees (. . .) The few snapshots I took during the march confirm my recollection of Teilhard's exhausted condition. But, although fatigue had robbed his whole figure of its wonderful poise and his face betrayed physical exhaustion, not a word of criticism or complaint escaped his lips. (*Helmut de Terra, 'Memories of Teilhard de Chardin'*)

On the Solo river, Java, 1938. Père Teilhard is seated in the centre

I visited the Ngandong area, which is rather inaccessible, saw the dome of Sangiran again (the site of the new Pithecanthropus) and the Karst area in the south (Patjitan) where there is a considerable industry. I had to leave before the end of the expedition, for I felt I was already late in getting back to Peking, so that I shall not be able to see the site of the baby-skull (near Surabaya). (*To the Abbé Breuil, 26 April 1938*)

Père Teilhard in Java

IN PEKING, MAY TO SEPTEMBER 1938, PÈRE TEILHARD BEGAN DRAFTING 'THE PHENOMENON OF MAN': 'IT SEEMS TO BE COMING ALONG NICELY'

I am working steadily on the first chapter of *The Phenomenon of Man*, a page or two a day. For the last ten months I have been thinking about it a great deal and it seemed to me that plan and inspiration had reached maturity. So far I have come up against no 'fault' as it develops. (*To Joseph Teilhard de Chardin, 5 August 1938*)

FROM NOVEMBER 1938 TO JUNE 1939 PÈRE TEILHARD DE CHARDIN WAS IN PARIS

Something deep and broad is obviously moving in the world, and in France especially (far behind the ridiculous political stage). For the last fortnight, I have been spending hours, almost every day, with the most extraordinary variety of people, ranging from the fringe of the working class up to the most refined, agnostic or sophisticated parts of society. Everywhere I find the birth, or at least the expectation, of the new creed of man in a spiritual evolution of the world. (*To Lucile Swan, 8 December 1938*)

Christmas 1938, in Paris. From left to right: Mrs. Evans, Mme. Ida Treat, Père Teilhard, Simone Bégouën, Max H. Bégouën

Père Teilhard at 'Études'

To have experienced and understood, in order to teach others to experience and understand, that all human enrichment is but dross except inasmuch as it becomes the most precious and incorruptible of all things by adding itself to an immortal centre of love: such is the supreme knowledge and the ultimate lesson to be imparted by the Christian educator. (*'Social Heredity and Progress', 1938, in 'The Future of Man'*)

In Paris, 1938

IN JUNE 1939, PÈRE TEILHARD SAILED FOR NEW YORK: THENCE BACK TO CHINA

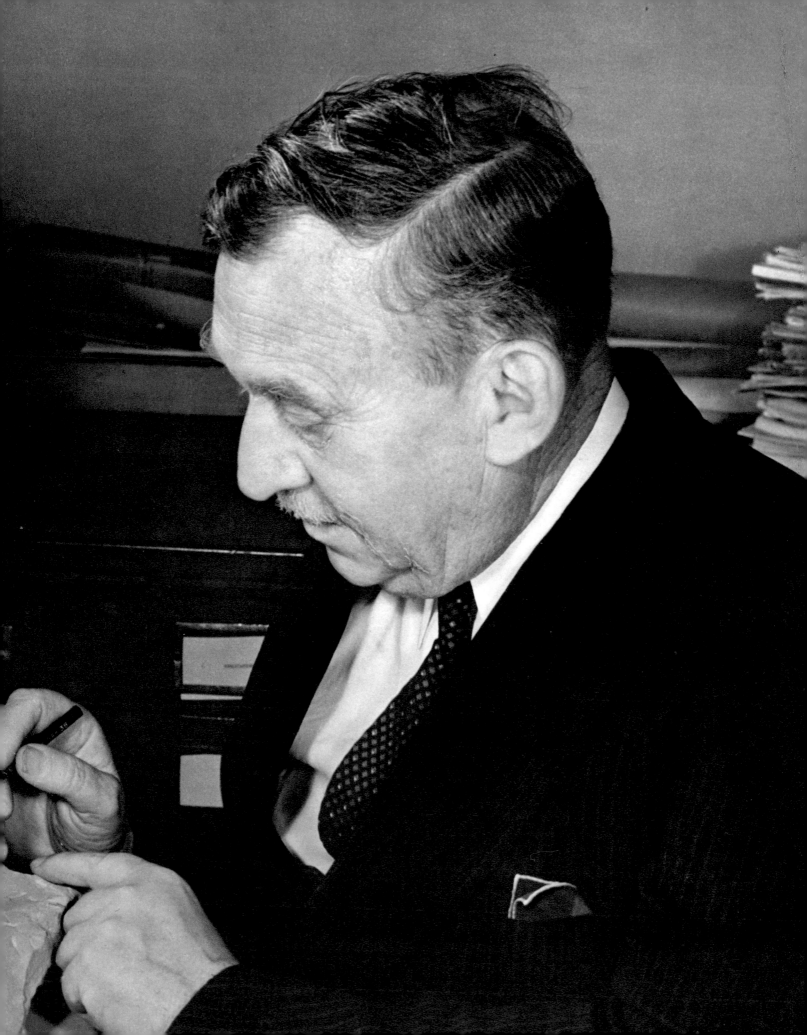

Père Teilhard in Peking, about 1941

Chapel of the Jesuit house, Chabanel Hall, Peking

1939–1945: PEKING

I arrived safely in Peking on August 30th. There were some physical inconveniences towards the end (a night on the floor at Tangku and eight hours in a crowded boat from Tangku to Tientsin); but that is no more than any traveller must expect as things are at present. I didn't stop at Tientsin, wisely as it turned out, for I could only have gone to the Hautes Études by boat (!), they'd have had some difficulty in putting me up (the house being full of refugees) and there was nothing I could have done. (*24 September 1939*)

Rickshaw in front of Chabanel Hall

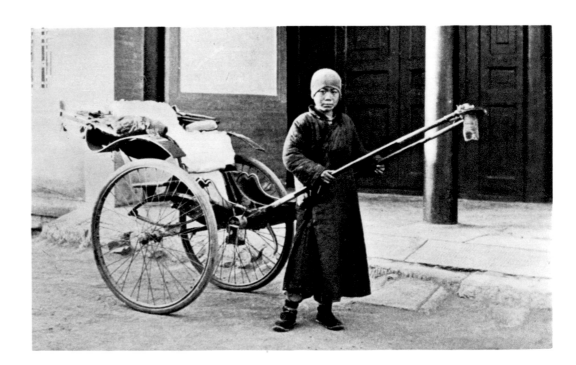

On preceding page:
Père Teilhard de Chardin and Dr. Walter Granger examining remains of fossilised birds in New York Museum of Natural History, July 1938

LIFE REMAINED UNRUFFLED IN PEKING, BUT PÈRE TEILHARD WAS HOMESICK FOR HIS NATIVE FRANCE

I am not sure when I last wrote to you. A long time ago, certainly—probably before the war started. This enormous event has disrupted all our plans, and I am waiting here. . . . I am still waiting to decide. Whatever way you look at it, it is obvious that the world is involved in a crisis of re-moulding, to which we must devote all our energies so that its new shape should accord with the Spirit of God and result in a new order closer to unity. But what, in my case, is the best course of action? And where should I apply it? (*To Jeanne Mortier, 7–8 December 1939*)

In Peking, 1940. On the left, Père Teilhard. On the right, Père Leroy

The Peking Union Medical College, where the palaeontological collections were housed

IN 1940, PÈRE TEILHARD, WITH HIS FRIEND PÈRE LEROY, FOUNDED THE INSTITUTE OF GEOBIOLOGY

So I continue to follow the routine of my two laboratories (...) The continental geology of China is gradually being sketched in; and *The Phenomenon of Man* progresses at the rate of a page or two a day (...) I feel that I have seldom worked so entirely for God alone. I am sure that He will give me the light and the strength to complete as it should be completed what I wish to say *only for Him*. (*To Max and Simone Bégouën, 8 February 1940*)

For many years now, I have had a sort of feeling that some form of action or external creation might be possible, which would give material expression in a tangible way, and in some organic form, to the ideas or attitudes that you share. And the more the years go by, the more I am coming to believe that my function will have been simply, like a very minor John the Baptist, to be the man who announces and summons what *must come about*. (*To Jeanne Mortier, 12 April 1940*)

Tea at Lucile Swan's

The outskirts of Peking

Well, on the first of May I entered my sixties. It's incredible how quickly time goes: my whole spiritual life consists more and more in abandoning myself (actively) to the presence and action of God. To be in communion with Becoming has become the formula of my whole life. (*To Claude Aragonnès, 19 May 1941*)

In the hills near Peking. From left to right: Père Teilhard de Chardin, Mme. Raphaël, Lucile Swan

On the outskirts of Peking

We're now in full spring. The pink of the apricot and peach trees, then the white of the apple trees, have gone like a dream, scattered by the dusty wind. Once or twice a week I have still been going to the Western Hills to do some field-work. (*To Gabriel and Joseph Teilhard de Chardin, 5 May 1941*)

Excursion into the Western Hills

Temple of the Azure Clouds,
Peking

Père Teilhard in Peking

Whatever the country, the creed or the social position of the person I approach, so long as the same fire of expectancy glows in him as it does in me, then a fundamental, final and total contact is immediately established. (*'La planétisation humaine, Peking, 25 December 1945*)

In Peking

AT THE BEGINNING OF MAY 1946, PÈRE TEILHARD DE CHARDIN RETURNED TO EUROPE

In Montsouris Park, during the palaeontological conference

PARIS, 17–23 APRIL 1947. PALAEONTOLOGICAL CONFERENCE ORGANISED BY PROFESSOR PIVETEAU, UNDER THE AEGIS OF THE CENTRE NATIONALE DE RECHERCHE SCIENTIFIQUE

Père Teilhard
during the conference

From left to right:
G. G. Simpson, Mrs. Haldane,
J. B. S. Haldane, Jean Viret,
D. M. S. Watson, Lucien Cuénot,
Mlle Dechaseaux, M. Guillaume,
Père Teilhard

In the library of
the Institute of Human Palaeontology

Père Teilhard speaking on the
evolution of the Siphnae

With backs to the camera,
from left to right:
Pierre Grassé, D. M. S. Watson,
G. G. Simpson, C. Arambourg,
M. Stensiö, Jean Piveteau

*Père Teilhard de Chardin and
Lucien Cuénot examining fossils
from the Far East, in the
Institute of Human Palaeontology*

Père Teilhard with D. M. S. Watson

In the early hours of 1st June a heart attack, which could have sent me to Jesus. Then a spell in hospital (rue Oudinot). And a turning-point in my life. The end of my work in the field. Today, at this very hour, I should have been in a plane on my way to Johannesburg. . . . What does it all mean? We shall see how it works out. Essentially, I can and will see only one meaning in it: being uprooted from the Cosmos in order to be more intimately, more really enveloped in Christianity—which is the *final* necessity in the Universe—and this at the price of a certain loss to science (which others will make good). . . . (*Personal note of 20 July 1947*)

When the signs of age begin to mark my body (and still more when they touch my mind); when the ill that is to diminish me or carry me off strikes from without or is born within me; when the painful moment comes in which I suddenly awaken to the fact that I am ill or growing old; and above all at that last moment when I feel I am losing hold of myself and am absolutely passive within the hands of the great unknown forces that have formed me; in all those dark moments, O God, grant that I may understand that it is You (provided only my faith is strong enough) who are painfully parting the fibres of my being in order to penetrate to the very marrow of my substance and bear me away within Yourself. ('*Le Milieu Divin*', 1926–7)

ON 25 JUNE 1947, PÈRE TEILHARD WAS PROMOTED TO THE RANK OF OFFICER OF THE LEGION OF HONOUR

At the instance of the Ministry of Foreign Affairs: 'for outstanding services to the intellectual and scientific influence of France, through a body of work mostly written and published in China, which has established him as a leading authority in international, and particularly in English-speaking, scientific circles. He may now be regarded, in the field of palaeontology and geology, as one of the chief ornaments of French science, whose international standing he has done much, by his personal contacts with foreign scientists, to maintain and exalt.'

Père Teilhard de Chardin, 1947

I still cannot measure the extent of the 'disaster', by which I mean to what extent serious field-work will still be possible. This I shall know in a few months' time. If the worst comes to the worst, I shall concentrate on intellectual work, which would fit in well enough with the logic of my life. In any case, I have decided to take this blow as a touch of the spur rather than a check from the bridle—if our Lord gives me the strength. (*To the Abbé Breuil, 15 July 1947*)

TWO MONTHS LATER, ROME FORBADE PÈRE TEILHARD TO PUBLISH

A week ago I had a letter from my General (Rome) forbidding me (in a perfectly courteous way) from publishing anything that involved philosophy or theology. And that neatly cuts out a large part of the activity still left open to me (...) All this isn't making life any brighter. Still, it is forcing me back upon 'the one thing that is necessary'. 'Everything that happens is worthy of worship,' Termier used to say. (*To the Abbé Breuil, 23 September 1947*)

The greater our power of manipulating inert and living matter, the greater proportionately must be our anxiety not to falsify or outrage any part of the reflective conscience that surrounds us. ('*The Human Rebound of Evolution and its Consequences*', *23 September 1947, in '*The Future of Man*')

Père Teilhard, in Paris, 1947

Père Teilhard in 1947

*Rome, the dome of St Peter's
seen from the Vatican gardens*

AUTUMN 1948. PÈRE TEILHARD LEFT FOR ROME TO MAKE A FINAL ATTEMPT TO OBTAIN PERMISSION
TO PUBLISH

I'm leaving this very evening for Rome, where I expect to stay until the
beginning of November. I have been invited there in a *very friendly spirit*.
We have to try to come to some agreement about the publication of my
book on *The Phenomenon of Man*. If, as I hope, it goes well, there's a good
chance that I may be given permission to stand for the Collège de France
(. . .) Whatever happens, however, I shall have had a chance to 'un-
burden my soul' by telling the supreme authority (in a friendly but perfectly open way) what seems to me to be the weakness, and also the
strength, of Christianity today. What a neo-humanism that looks to the
future must have is nothing less than a more profound Christianity, re-
thought to fit the new dimensions of the world. (*To George Barbour,
2 October 1948*)

O Jesus, let me end well—that is, in a gesture of testimony to seal my
life's assertion and faith in a Pole of love in the universal drift. Through
Death, Communion (the Communion of Death) . . .

Pray that I may end well . . . that is the grace of all graces—particularly
when one has taken it on oneself, in however humble a way, to point out
the road to others. (*To Père d'Ouince, 24 October 1948*)

*The Château of Les Moulins,
Neuville (Puy-de-Dôme), home
of Joseph Teilhard de Chardin*

EVERY SUMMER, PÈRE TEILHARD DE CHARDIN WENT FOR A REST TO LES MOULINS, WHERE HE
MADE HIS ANNUAL RETREAT. IT WAS THERE THAT IN SEPTEMBER 1948 HE FINISHED 'COMMENT
JE VOIS', AND IN 1950 'LE COEUR DE LA MATIÈRE'

Père Teilhard at Sarcenat

IN AUGUST 1949,
HE RECEIVED A VISIT FROM GEORGE BARBOUR

We spent two unforgettable days, strolling down the
avenues, sitting in the garden, listening to him talking
about his childhood with Marguerite, about the danger to
the vines from hailstorms, and how the vinegrowers were
benefiting from the weather forecasts, about his slow con-
valescence, and about the encouragement of his friend-
ships. Had we heard the latest news from China? Which
of his friends had I met in London? Would I have known,
without being told, that Joseph was his brother? Would I
be sure, when I was back in Paris, to go and see the Abbé
Breuil and give him love from Les Moulins? And could I,
in two years' time, visit Africa again? *George Barbour,
'Teilhard de Chardin in the Field')*

182

Australopithecus sites in Southern Africa

Evolution, which offers a passage to something that escapes total death, is the hand of God drawing us to himself. (*'La Biologie, poussée à fond, peut-elle nous conduire à émerger dans le transcendant?'*, *May 1951*)

SUMMER 1951. FIRST VISIT TO SOUTH AFRICA

I am setting off with a much more precise idea of my two-fold objective (the Australopithecus and the ultra-human) and with plenty to think round and about during the voyage. All this is directed towards the search for the 'ever-greater God', for ultimately it is only the pull towards Him that is sending me on this new—perhaps my last?—adventure. (*To Claude Aragonnès, from Southampton, 11 July 1951*)

I feel that things are turning out well. I can see the problems more clearly, and I have a pretty good idea of what will be the substance of my report to Fejos. And at the same time as the question of 'pre-man' is taking shape in my mind, my ideas on the other question—that of the 'ultra-human'—continue to make progress. (*To Claude Aragonnès, 13 August 1951*)

My first impressions of the possibilities of work in South Africa, as regards the discovery of bone remains of the first men, are *good*. In my opinion, three main lines of research, as things are, are open for an immediate campaign.

A. The most important of all is to continue the investigation of the Australopithecus site at Sterkfontein (combined with laboratory preparation of the non-Primate fossils unearthed by the late Dr. Broom). My chief task will be to reconnoitre, with the assistance of Robinson, the most promising aspects of the area.

Dr. Broom examining in situ the Plesianthropus skull he found at Sterkfontein

Père Teilhard at Sterkfontein

186

*Dr. van Riet Lowe and
Père Teilhard at Makapan*

**REPORT TO DR. FEJOS,
CONTINUED**

B. Almost equally important, I am sure, is to complete the diggings in
the remarkable Makapan site located by Dr. van Riet Lowe. In this little
South African Chou-Kou-Tien (which contains, in a hard breccia, typical
coups de poing and a rich fauna) there should be a good chance of finding
bones of Early Pleistocene Man of South Africa. I am planning to visit
the site this month. Apparently the work of excavation could be completed in a fairly short time at relatively moderate expense.

Père Teilhard at Makapan

Père Teilhard de Chardin and
Dr. van Riet Lowe at Makapan

The local geologists and prehistorians here are charming. In their company, and thanks to their kindness, I have already begun to visit the most interesting of the sites. Last week I was at Makapan, some 180 miles north from here. It was a four-day trip and most rewarding. (*To Joseph Teilhard de Chardin, 18 August 1951*)

View of the Makapan excavations, sketch by van Riet Lowe in Père Teilhard's notebook

c. Quite recently an open site (consolidated sand-dunes) has been found by the sea, some 100 miles north of Capetown. Here heavily fossilised remains of elephant, rhino, horse and ruminants are associated with *coups de poing* (and also with Upper Palaeolithic implements: probably from two strata). This locality might provide us with a surface equivalent of the Makapan cave deposits and should therefore be studied closely. (*To Paul Fejos, 1 August 1951*)

In South Africa, 1951

Taungs, Australopithecus site visited by Père Teilhard at the end of August 1951

. . . One could well say that today, as was the case in Galilee, what we most need if we are to recognise the convergence of the universe is not so much new facts (there are enough, and even embarrassingly more than enough, of these everywhere) as a new way of looking at and handling facts.

A new way of seeing, combined with a new way of acting: that is what we need.

(. . .) What we have to do is to make up our minds and get to work—*quickly, right now. ('La convergence de l'univers', 23 July 1951)*

Dr. B. Malan, Pére Teilhard de Chardin and Dr. van Riet Lowe

In South Africa, 1951

The Wenner-Gren Foundation for Anthropological Research. Père Teilhard's office was on the fourth floor, the right-hand window

RETURNING IN NOVEMBER 1951 TO NEW YORK, PÈRE TEILHARD FOUND THAT HIS VISIT WAS TO BECOME A PERMANENT RESIDENCE

I gather from the new Provincial at Lyons that the situation at Rome, as far as I am concerned, is rather strained. . . . It so happens that Dr. Fejos, the director of research at the Wenner-Gren Foundation which sent me to Africa . . . is asking me (as a favour!) to join him as a 'research associate'. . . . I am not sure what will happen in the end. But everything is turning out so curiously for me, as in 1923 when China was waiting for me when I arrived from Paris. This time it's America, and I am 70' (*To Jeanne Mortier, 30 November 1951*)

The Chapel of the Sacred Heart, St Ignatius's, New York, where Père Teilhard liked to say Mass

Yes, I hope that the Lord will use us as much as possible in the great task of bringing 'the Christ of today' to the world of today. I was thinking again this morning of the profound difference that divides the two ways of understanding both 'the heart' and 'the Cross' of Jesus. You can see it simply as a suffering 'Heart' to be 'consoled'. Or you can see it as a centre of energy that creates and drives the world: it suffers, indeed, but it is even more a fire, the only fire that can keep in motion a universe that has become reflective. (*To Jeanne Mortier, 20 June 1952*)

Garden of St Ignatius's, New York

SUMMER 1952. PÈRE TEILHARD'S SCIENTIFIC JOURNEY IN THE WESTERN STATES

My stay at the Simpsons (George Gaylord, the palaeontologist) was most agreeable and picturesque. They live—he and his wife—8,000 feet up, on the edge of a national park, three hours by car from Albuquerque, looking right over the Bad Lands of the San Juan basin. (This winter wild turkeys were pecking for food around the house.) I slept in a tent (...) In a few hours, I learnt a great deal of geology and firmly cemented my friendship with both the Simpsons. (*To Père Leroy, 12 July 1952*)

* Collenia: calcareous precipitations caused by the action of algae

At Glacial Park (Montana, on the Canadian border) I was able to see all the *Collenia** I wanted, thanks to the kindness of the chief naturalist and to the fortunate presence of a young geologist from the National Survey who is at the moment studying the problem of *Collenia*. I am going to send some notes about it (as compared with China and the Transvaal) to the Geological Society of France and the Institut. Wonderful weather, fortunately—and a country of huge mountains and forests. (*To Père Leroy, 9 September 1952*)

Père Teilhard de Chardin at
Glacial Park (Montana) in 1952

195

At Hopefield, 1953

TEILHARD, SENT BY THE WENNER GREN FOUNDATION, MEETS A. G. H. GOODWIN AT CAPETOWN

We spent five days at Capetown (time to see the markedly Neanderthaloid skull-cap found this year in the consolidated, fossiliferous sanddunes of Hopefield—and to discuss further work at Hopefield). (*To Père Leroy, 5 August 1953*)

Père Teilhard de Chardin with Professor Goodwin, of Capetown

Père Teilhard de Chardin at Hopefield, 1953

In the African bush

Finally, all that I have seen and heard (. . .) confirms me in the idea that *I did well* to come. I have arrived just at the time when research into human origins is being reorganised and has received a new impetus—and that in a critical region of the earth. I believe that I can be of some use in this field, in organising and inspiring. In any case, I am learning a great deal—and ideas are coming. All I now have to do is continually to put my trust more completely in the guiding influence of the 'Milieu Divin'. (*To Jeanne Mortier, 30 July 1953*)

AT THE END OF AUGUST, PÈRE TEILHARD VISITED THE VICTORIA FALLS, ZAMBESI RIVER

Apart from the large fauna, which have disappeared except in the reserves, the country can hardly have changed since Livingstone's day—vast rolling expanses covered with bush in which most of the various trees are as tall as the average oak. It's the end of the dry season: a background of tall yellow grasses and bare branches, but quite a few green trees as well. I saw two big rivers: the Kafue, near Lusaka, and right where I am now the majestic and historic Zambesi, with its magnificent falls which I can hear at the moment. These Victoria Falls, though they are in Southern Rhodesia, are only five miles from Livingstone. The day before yesterday Clark took us for a picnic with his family above the falls in a motor-launch. (*To Joseph Teilhard de Chardin, 2 September 1953*)

In the Cave of the Hearths, Makapan.
From left to right: Peter van Riet Lowe,
Père Teilhard de Chardin, and Revil Mason

On the whole, I am extremely interested by all that I see: both from the general viewpoint of human origins, and from the particular point of view of the strategy to follow in order to mount a general attack on Africa south of the Sahara. With a good 'five-year plan' (to which I hope to convert Fejos) it should be possible to establish at Makapan an ascending series of super-imposed deposits running from the Australopithecine layers (...) to the Upper Palaeolithic (inclusive). With two or three similar points (of which we have Hopefield, near Capetown, and Olduvai in Tanganyika). (*To Père Leroy, 5 August 1953*)

Dr. Leakey at Olduvai

The Olduvai Gorges, Tanganyika,
where some years later Dr. Leakey
made some important finds

Near Lusaka, Desmond Clark showed me *Freeman's Hole* (where we found several other broken pebbles *in situ*) and the breccia of the Twin River (where we—that is to say Clark—extracted the other half of the implement you and he had found and broken some months ago). (*To Professor Oakley, 28 November 1953*)

At the point we have reached in our knowledge of general palaeontology, it seems surprising that Africa was not immediately identified as the only region in the world where the first traces of the human species could be sought with any chances of success. (*Address given by Père Teilhard at New York, after his return from Johannesburg. 'Africa and human origins', published in 'The Appearance of Man'*)

Père Teilhard de Chardin at the entrance to Freeman's Hole, Kafue Gorge, Northern Rhodesia

Père Teilhard de Chardin examining a stone implement, in Northern Rhodesia

RETURN TO NEW YORK, AFTER PUTTING IN AT BUENOS AIRES

And now life starts again in this great New York that I am decidedly very fond of (. . .) I have never felt so vividly that all strength and all inspirations come from God. (*To Solange Lemaître, 11 November 1953*)

My first task on getting here has been to get some scientific papers finished (a piece for the Academy and a short article for Vaufrey and *Anthropology*). And now, with you in mind, I am going to tidy up two short articles I drafted out on the journey: one is called 'The Stuff of the Universe' and the other 'The God of Evolution'. (*To Jeanne Mortier, 11 November 1953*)

New York, view from the American
Museum of Natural History

SUMMER 1954. PÈRE TEILHARD'S LAST VISIT TO FRANCE

Lord of my childhood and Lord of my end—God complete in himself, and yet, for us, continually being born (. . .), sweep away at last all the clouds that still shroud you—the clouds of hostile prejudice and the clouds of false belief. And, through what is at once diaphany and conflagration, may your Universal Presence leap forth. O Christ, ever more great. ('*Le Coeur de la Matière*', *1950*)

The Château of Sarcenat, to which Père Teilhard
paid a flying visit during his last days in France

I can retain nothing from this too hasty visit to Paris except a mass of more or less chaotic impressions: nevertheless a few clear, or clarified points do stand out.

1. That, through all that is most vital in me, I feel that I am more and more dedicated to my vocation of devoting my life—what remains of my life—to the discovery and the service of the Universal Christ. 2. That— for the immediate future at least—it is most certainly in shadow and exile that I must work. (*To Jeanne Mortier, 22 September 1954*)

Into what lies ahead. . . life's last withdrawal
APPROPINQUAT HORA CHRISTI
(*Notes in retreat, 1954*)

The country house of Strauss, the publisher, at Purchase, where Père Teilhard de Chardin made his last retreats

The American Museum of Natural History, seen from Central Park

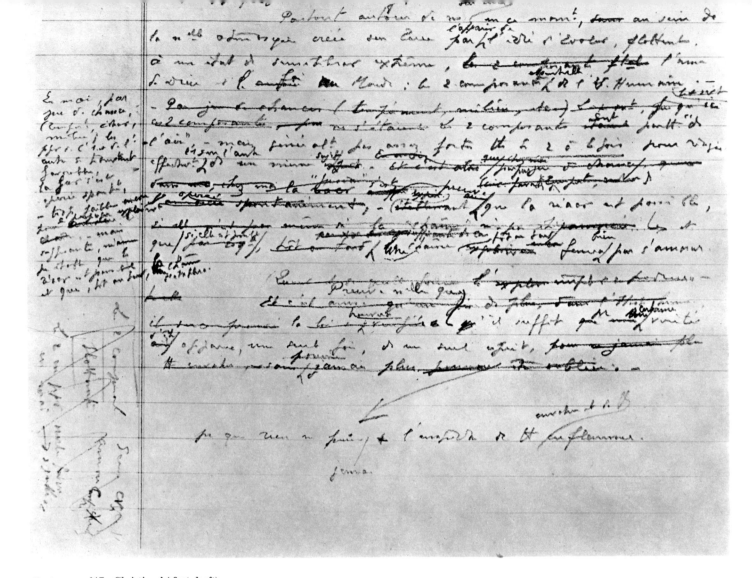

Last page of 'Le Christique' (first draft)

IN MARCH 1955 PÈRE TEILHARD DE CHARDIN CROWNED FOUR YEARS OF INTENSE WORK WITH
HIS SPIRITUAL TESTAMENT: 'LE CHRISTIQUE'

Everywhere on earth, at this moment, within the new spiritual atmosphere created by the appearance of the idea of evolution, there float—in a state of extreme mutual sensitivity—the two essential components of the Ultra-human, love of God and faith in the world. Everywhere these two components are 'in the air': generally, however, they are not strong enough, *both at the same time*, to combine with one another *in one and the same subject*. In me, by pure chance (temperament, education, environment) the proportion of each happens to be favourable, and they fuse together spontaneously. The fusion of the two is still not strong enough to spread explosively, but even so it is enough to show that such an explosion is possible and that, *sooner or later the chain-reaction will get under way*.

It is one more proof that if the truth appears once, in one single mind, that is enough to ensure that nothing can ever prevent it from spreading to everything and setting it ablaze. (*'Le Christique'*, *March 1955*)

*On the preceding page, Manhattan
in spring, seen from the American
Museum of Natural History*

*Père Teilhard de Chardin
in New York, 1955*

God must, in some way or other, make room for himself, hollowing us out and emptying us, if he is finally to penetrate into us. And in order to assimilate us in him, he must break the molecules of our being so as to re-cast and re-model us. The function of death is to provide the necessary entrance into our inmost selves. It will make us undergo the required dissociation. It will put us into the state organically needed if the divine fire is to descend upon us. And in that way its fatal power to decompose and dissolve will be harnessed to the most sublime operations of life. (*'Le Milieu Divin'*, *1926–7*)

Energy becoming Presence . . .

One would think that a single ray of this kind of light, falling anywhere on the Noosphere, as a spark, would cause an explosion strong enough to inflame and transform the face of Earth almost instantaneously. How then can it be that I, looking around me, still intoxicated by what has been shown to me, should find myself alone, as it were, the only one of my species? The only one to have *seen*? . . . and so unable, when asked, to cite a single author, a single text, which might clearly describe the marvellous 'Translucence' that has so transfigured everything I see? (*'The Christique'*, *March 1955*)

I should like to die on the day of the Resurrection. (Père Teilhard's words at a dinner at the French Consulate in New York, 15 March 1954, noted at the time by one of his nephews)

ON EASTER SUNDAY, 10 APRIL 1955, PÈRE TEILHARD DE CHARDIN DIED IN NEW YORK

Lord, since with every instinct of my being and through all the changing fortunes of my life, it is You whom I have ever sought, You whom I have set at the heart of universal matter, it will be in a resplendence which shines through all things and in which all things are ablaze, that I shall have the felicity of closing my eyes. (*'Le Coeur de la Matière, 1950*)

The last photograph of Père Teilhard de Chardin

Principal Dates

DATES	PRINCIPAL EVENTS	JOURNEYS AND PLACES	MAJOR WORKS AND THOSE QUOTED IN ALBUM
1875 18 MAY	Emmanuel Teilhard de Chardin marries Berthe-Adèle de Dompierre d'Hornoy		
1881 1 MAY	Marie-Joseph Pierre Teilhard de Chardin born	Sarcenat	
1897	Passes baccalauréat examination in philosophy		
1898	Passes baccalauréat in mathematics		
1899 20 MARCH	Enters Jesuit noviciate	Aix-en-Provence	
1900 SEPTEMBER	First year of juniorate	Laval	
1901 25 MARCH	Simple vows	Laval	
OCTOBER	Second year of juniorate	Jersey	
1902	Graduates Licence ès lettres	Caen	
27 SEPTEMBER	Death of Albéric, Teilhard's elder brother		
OCTOBER	First year as a scholastic Geological field trips in Jersey	Jersey	
1904 AUGUST	Death of Teilhard's sister, Louise		
1905 END OF AUGUST	Leaves for Egypt for required three years' teaching in Jesuit college	Cairo	
1906 AUGUST	Geological field trip	Jebel Mokattem	
1907 APRIL	Geological field trip	Faiyum	
DECEMBER			*Huit jours au Fayoum*
1908 JANUARY	Geological field trip	Upper Egypt	
1909 OCTOBER	First year of theology Geological field trip with Père Pellotier	Hastings The Weald; Jersey	*L'éocène des environs de Minieh*
1910			*Notes sur les roches éruptives de Jersey*
1911 7 JUNE	Teilhard's sister, Françoise, dies in China		
24 AUGUST	Ordained priest	Hastings	
1912	Continues theological studies		
3 SEPTEMBER	Attends Conference on Religious Ethnology	Louvain	
OCTOBER	Begins course under Marcellin Boule at the Museum of Natural History Studies phosphorites in Quercy	Paris	
NOVEMBER			*Pour fixer les traits d'un monde qui s'efface*
1913 JANUARY			*The Progress of Prehistory (The Appearance of Man)*
JUNE–JULY	Scientific trip to Spain with Abbé Breuil and Fr. Hugo Obermaier	Santander Altamira	
1914 JULY	Field trip with Jean Boussac	Alpes du Dauphiné	
AUGUST	Begins tertianship	Canterbury	
12 NOVEMBER	Teilhard's brother, Gonzague, is killed in action		
DECEMBER	Called up for service with medical corps	Clermont	*Les carnassiers des phosphorites du Quercy*
1915 JANUARY	Stretcher-bearer (2nd class) in the 8th Moroccan Light Infantry		
MAY		Ypres Sector	

DATES	PRINCIPAL EVENTS	JOURNEYS AND PLACES	MAJOR WORKS AND THOSE QUOTED IN ALBUM
JUNE	Transfers to 4th combined regiment of Zouaves and Light Infantry		
AUGUST		Arras district	
29 AUGUST	Mentioned in divisional orders		
1 SEPTEMBER	Croix de Guerre		
1916 JANUARY	In billets behind the line	Nieuport-Ville	
24 MARCH	From this date onwards drafts numerous writings		*La vie cosmique* (*Écrits guerre*)
24 APRIL	Finishes *La vie cosmique*	Dunkirk sector	
17 SEPTEMBER	Mentioned in army orders		*Christ in the World of Matter: Three stories in the style of Benson* (*Hymn of the Universe*).
14 OCTOBER			
24 OCTOBER	Fortress at Douamont retaken by Teilhard's regiment.	Verdun sector	
1917 13 JANUARY	Promoted to honorary stretcher-bearer	Boviolles (Meuse)	
20 JUNE	Awarded Médaille Militaire		
13 AUGUST		Beaulieu-les-Fontaines	*Le milieu mystique*
OCTOBER		Chemin des Dames	(*Écrits guerre*)
1918 JANUARY		Mourmelon	
15 FEBRUARY		Vertus	*La grande monade* (*Écrits guerre*)
14 APRIL		Ay-sur-Marne	*Mon univers* (*Écrits guerre*)
3 MAY	Teilhard's brother, Olivier, is killed at Mount Kemmel		
26 MAY	Takes solemn vows	Ste-Foy-lès-Lyon	
8 JULY		Compiègne district	*Le prêtre* (*Écrits guerre*)
28 SEPTEMBER		Montbéliard area	*La foi qui opère* (*Écrits guerre*)
1919 8 JANUARY		Strasbourg	(*Écrits guerre. Note pour servir à l'évangelisation des temps nouveaux*
JULY	Passes certificate in geology	Paris	*The Spiritual Power of Matter*
8 AUGUST		Jersey	(*Hymn of the Universe*)
OCTOBER	Passes certificate in botany	Paris	
1920 MARCH	Passes certificate in zoology	Paris	
JUNE	Preparation of doctoral thesis in geology at the Institut Catholique		
JULY	Excavations near Rheims in connection with thesis	Rheims	
10 AUGUST		Paris	*A Note on Progress* (*The Future of Man*)
1921 FEBRUARY			*Science et Christ*
MARCH	Reviews Marcellin Boule's book on fossil men in *Études*		*Fossil Men* (*The Appearance of Man*)
21 MAY	Chevalier de la Légion d'Honneur		
1922 22 MARCH	Oral examination for doctoral thesis Assistant Professor of Geology		*Les mammifères de l'éocène inférieur français*
1923 6 APRIL	To China via Suez, Ceylon, Sumatra, Hong Kong, Shanghai		
MAY	Joins Père Emile Licent, S.J.	Tientsin	
JUNE	First field trip with Licent	Ordos	
6 AUGUST	Writes *Mass on the World* in the Ordos Desert		
OCTOBER		Tientsin	
DECEMBER			*The Mass on the World* (*Hymn of the Universe*)
1924 FEBRUARY	Visits Jesuit mission centre at Sien-Hsien	Cheli	
25 MARCH		Tientsin	*Mon univers*
APRIL	Field trip with Père Licent	Eastern Mongolia	
JUNE		Dalai-Nor (Tari N.)	
AUGUST	Joins Professor George Barbour	Kalgan	
SEPTEMBER	Returns to France by sea	Shanghai	
OCTOBER	Resumes courses at Institut Catholique Gives retreats for students of Grandes Écoles	Paris	

DATES	PRINCIPAL EVENTS	JOURNEYS AND PLACES	MAJOR WORKS AND THOSE QUOTED IN ALBUM
1925 MAY	Posting abroad at express direction of superiors		
1926 APRIL	Leaves for China with Père Licent and Père Lejay		
SPRING	Travelling	Shensi, Shansi	
NOVEMBER	Drafts treatise on spirituality	Tientsin	*Le milieu divin*
DECEMBER	Visited by Professor Alfred Lacroix of the Museum of Natural History	Peking	
1927 MAY-JULY	Field trip with Licent	Dalai-Nor (Tari N.)	
AUGUST	Back in France		
1928 AUGUST	Stays with family and with friends	Le Chambon (Auvergne) Les Espas (Ariège)	*Le phénomène humain*
NOVEMBER	Trip to Africa with Henri de Monfreid and Pierre Lamare, the geologist	Somaliland, Ethiopia	
1929 FEBRUARY	Return to China via Jibuti and Ceylon		*Le sens humain*
MARCH		Tientsin	
APRIL	Accepts post as scientific adviser to Peking Geological Service. Lives with Lazarist Fathers. Works with Dr. Davidson Black and Dr. Wong Wen Hao at Chou-Kou-Tien		
MAY	Final field trip with Père Licent Trip on Trans-Siberian Railway	Manchuria Dalai-Nor (Hulun N.)	
JULY-AUGUST	Field trip for Chinese Geological Service	Shansi	
OCTOBER	With George Barbour, Black and Wong	Chou-Kou-Tien	*Rapport sur les dépôts fossilères de Chou-Kou-Tien (with C. C. Young)*
2 DECEMBER	Pei-Wen-Chung, Director of Excavations at Chou-Kou-Tien, discovers the first Sinanthropus skull		
1930 JANUARY		Tientsin	*The Phenomenon of Man (essay in Vision of the Past)*
FEBRUARY	Trip with Barbour	Shensi, Shansi	
APRIL		Peking	*Sinanthropus Pekinensis*
MAY	Joins Chapman Andrews expedition	Mongolia, Gobi Desert	
AUGUST		Peking	
SEPTEMBER	Return to France	Paris	
DECEMBER	Lectures to Marcel Légaut's group in Auvergne	Chadefaud	
1931 JANUARY	Trip to U.S.A. to make arrangements for Citroën expedition	New York, Chicago	
FEBRUARY	Return to China via Hawaii and Japan	San Francisco	
MARCH	Waiting to join Yellow Expedition	Peking	*Le Sinanthropus de Pékin* *The Spirit of the Earth (Building the Earth)*
8 MAY	Joins expedition	Kalgan, Gobi Desert	
JUNE		Black Gobi Etsin-Gol Valley	
28 JUNE	Battle of Khami	Khami	
19 JULY	Expedition taken prisoner by Chinese	Urumchi	
6 SEPTEMBER	Leaves with a small group to meet Haardt		
8 OCTOBER	The two groups link up	Aksu	
23 OCTOBER	Visits dead cities in Gobi Desert	Bäzäklik	
27 OCTOBER	Return to camp	Urumchi	
23 NOVEMBER	Departure from camp	Gobi Desert	
1932 1 JANUARY	With the Divine Word Fathers	Liangchow (Kansu)	
11 FEBRUARY	Death of Teilhard's father		
12 FEBRUARY	Return of Yellow Expedition	Peking	
JULY	Travelling	Shansi	
SEPTEMBER	Return to France for four months Contacts with religious and scientific circles	Paris	
25 DECEMBER		London	
1933 END OF JANUARY	Talk on the meaning of suffering to Catholic Union of the Sick	Paris	
FEBRUARY	Leaves for fifth journey to China		

DATES	PRINCIPAL EVENTS	JOURNEYS AND PLACES	MAJOR WORKS AND THOSE QUOTED IN ALBUM
MARCH		Peking	
APRIL			*Signification de la souffrance*
JULY	Trip to U.S.A. via Pacific route	San Francisco	
	Attends International Congress of Geology in Washington	Washington, New York	
SEPTEMBER	Trips in California	Nevada, Grand Canyon	
NOVEMBER	Return to China by Pacific route	Peking	
1934 MARCH	Death of Davidson Black		
MAY	Yangtze Expedition, and trip to Central Asia with Barbour	Yangtze Honan, Tsinling Mts	
AUGUST	Return of expedition	Peking	
OCTOBER	Death of Teilhard's brother, Victor		*Comment je crois*
28 OCTOBER			
1935 JANUARY	Leaves for South China with Wong and Pei	Koang-si, Koang-tong	
MARCH	Visited by Abbé Breuil	Peking	
MAY	Return to France	Paris	
SEPTEMBER	Departure for India to join Helmut de Terra	Red Sea Kashmir	*The Discovery of the Past* (*Vision of the Past*)
OCTOBER		Salt Range	
DECEMBER		Narbada Valley	
END OF DECEMBER	To Java at invitation of Von Koenigswald	Batavia, Bandung, Sangiran	
1936 JANUARY	Return to China via Hong Kong and Shanghai	Peking	
7 FEBRUARY	Teilhard's mother dies		
4 MAY		Peking	*Esquisse d'un univers personnel*
JULY	Travelling	Shantung	
17 AUGUST	Teilhard's sister, Marie, dies		
SEPTEMBER		Tientsin	
OCTOBER		Peking	
NOVEMBER			*We must save mankind* (*Building the Earth*)
1937 FEBRUARY	Trip to U.S.A. across Pacific via Honolulu	Philadelphia	*Le phénomène spirituel*
MARCH	Awarded Gregor Mendel Medal at Philadelphia Conference		
APRIL	Return to France via Atlantic route	New York	
19 APRIL	Arrival in France	Paris	
JULY	Spent on his brother Joseph's estate	Les Moulins, Neuville	
6 AUGUST	Leaves for China from Marseilles on board the D'Artagnan		*Human Energy* (*Building the Earth*)
18 SEPTEMBER	Arrival in China	Tientsin	
DECEMBER	To Burma to join Helmut de Terra	Rangoon	
1938 JANUARY		Shan Plateau from the Irrawaddy	
MARCH	Arrival in Java with Helmut de Terra; stays with Von Koenigswald	Batavia, Bandung, Surakarta, Trinil, La Solo	
MAY	Return to China	Peking	
JUNE	Begins *The Phenomenon of Man*		
SEPTEMBER	Leaves for U.S.A. via Pacific route	Vancouver, New York	
NOVEMBER	Returns to France via Atlantic route		*Social Heredity and Progress* (*The Future of Man*)
25 DECEMBER	Christmas with the Bégouëns	Paris	
1939 20 MARCH		Paris	*La mystique de la science*
24-31 MARCH	Trip to England	London	
JUNE	Return to China via U.S.A.		
JULY		New York, Chicago, San Francisco	
AUGUST	Sails for China	Vancouver	
30 AUGUST	Arrival in China where he stays until 1946	Peking	
DECEMBER			*L'heure de choisir*

DATES	PRINCIPAL EVENTS	JOURNEYS AND PLACES	MAJOR WORKS AND THOSE QUOTED IN ALBUM
1940 MAY	Sets up Institute of Geobiology with Père Pierre Leroy, S.J.		
JUNE	Finishes *The Phenomenon of Man*		*The Phenomenon of Man*
SEPTEMBER	Publishes several papers on Chou-Kou-Tien		*The Granitization of China*
31 OCTOBER			*La parole attendue*
1941 3 MARCH	Lectures at French Embassy on 'The Future of Man as seen by a Paleontologist'		*Some Reflections on Progress (The Future of Man)*
OCTOBER	His brother, Gabriel, dies		
DECEMBER			*Early Man in China*
1942 OCTOBER		Peking	*Le Christ évoluteur*
15 NOVEMBER	Exposition of law of complexity—consciousness		*Man's Place in the Universe (The Vision of the Past)*
END OF NOVEMBER	Travelling	Shanghai	
1943	Founds journal *Geobiologia*	Peking	
AUGUST			*Super humanité, super Christ*
28 DECEMBER			*Réflexions sur le bonheur*
1944 AUGUST	Working with Pei		*Le néolithique de la Chine*
DECEMBER			*La centrologie*
1945 JUNE			*Life and the Planets (The Future of Man)*
AUGUST			*Action et activation*
1946 MAY	In France. Various activities, including lectures	Paris	
SEPTEMBER			*Some Reflections on the Spiritual Repercussions of the Atom Bomb (The Future of Man)*
NOVEMBER			*Esquisse d'une dialectique de l'esprit*
1947 FEBRUARY		Paris	*Apport spirituel de l'Extrême-Orient*
APRIL	Symposium on Paleontology and Genetics	Paris	
1 JUNE	Heart attack	Paris	
25 JUNE	Officier de la Légion d'Honneur Convalescence at clinic of Augustinian Nuns of the Immaculate Conception	St.-Germain-en-Laye	
SEPTEMBER			*The Human Rebound of Evolution (The Future of Man)*
1948 MARCH	Sixth trip to U.S.A.	New York	
JUNE	Return to France	Paris	
AUGUST	Stays with his brother, Joseph	Les Moulins	*Comment je vois*
SEPTEMBER	Lecture at Versailles on modern neo-humanism		
OCTOBER	Seeks ecclesiastical approval for publication of *The Phenomenon of Man* and for appointment to Chair at Collège de France	Rome	
NOVEMBER	Return to France after negative response to both requests	Paris	
1949 FEBRUARY	Lectures at Sorbonne on *Groupe Zoologique humain*	Paris	
MARCH	Attack of pleurisy	Paris	
APRIL-MAY	Convalescence at Augustinian Nuns' clinic	St-Germain-en-Laye	
MAY			*Does mankind move biologically upon itself? (The Future of Man)*
4 AUGUST	Completes *Man's Place in Nature*	Paris	
AUGUST	Stays with his brother, Joseph	Les Moulins	*Man's Place in Nature*
SEPTEMBER		Paris	
OCTOBER	Attends International Congress on Philosophy of Science	Paris	*The Vision of our Past (The Vision of the Past)*
1950 JANUARY			*Énergie spirituel de la souffrance*

DATES	PRINCIPAL EVENTS	JOURNEYS AND PLACES	MAJOR WORKS AND THOSE QUOTED IN ALBUM
APRIL			*From the Pre-Human to the Ultra-Human (The Future of Man)*
MAY	Elected non-resident member of Académie des Sciences (Institut de France)		*Le phénomène chrétien*
15 AUGUST	Stays with his brother, Joseph	Les Moulins	*Le Cœur de la matière*
	Visited by Barbour	Les Moulins	
OCTOBER	Lectures in Belgium	Liége, Brussels	
NOVEMBER		Paris	*Le goût de vivre*
1951 MARCH			*Du cosmos à la cosmogénèse*
MAY	Attends Conference of Catholic Intellectuals	Paris	*La biologie, poussée à fond . . .*
JULY	Leaves for South Africa. Breaks journey in England, joins Barbour. Barbour flies to South Africa, Teilhard sails from Southampton	London	
23 JULY		Cape Town	*La convergence de l'univers*
28 AUGUST	Visits sites of Australopithecus, finds with Barbour and van Riet Lowe	Johannesburg, Pretoria, Kimberley Dry Harts Valley	
SEPTEMBER		Johannesburg, Durban	
OCTOBER	Visits Hopefield site with Dr. J. Goodwin	Cape Town	
NOVEMBER	Return to U.S.A. via Buenos Aires and Rio de Janeiro	New York	
DECEMBER	Accepts research post with Wenner Gren Foundation offered by Dr. Paul Fejos		
30 DECEMBER			*Hominization and Speciation (Vision of the Past)*
1952 APRIL			*La réflexion de l'énergie*
JULY	Trip across U.S.A.	Chicago	
	Stays with Prof. George Gaylord Simpson	Rocky Mountains	
	Visits cyclotron at Berkeley	California	
	Visits Glacier Park on return trip	Montana	
SEPTEMBER		New York	*Ce que le monde attend de l'Église de Dieu*
DECEMBER	Christmas in New York		
1953 JANUARY		New York	*Sur la compression humaine*
APRIL			*En regardant un cyclotron*
MAY			*L'énergie d'évolution*
JUNE			*La multiplicité des mondes habités*
JULY	Second South African trip		*L'étoffe de l'univers*
18 JULY	Visits Hopefield and Australopithecus sites	Cape Town, Johannesburg, Pretoria	
END OF AUGUST	Flies to Northern Rhodesia	Livingstone, The Zambezi	
SEPTEMBER	Return to South Africa	Pretoria	
OCTOBER	Return to U.S.A. via Rio and Trinidad	Equator,	*Le Dieu de l'évolution*
NOVEMBER		New York	
DECEMBER			*L'activation de l'énergie humaine*
1954 MARCH		New York	*The Singularities of the Human Species (The Appearance of Man)*
JUNE	In France	Paris	
28 JUNE	Lecture on Africa and origins of man	Paris	
JULY	Visits Lascaux with Père Leroy	Lascaux	
	Last visit to birthplace	Sarcenat	
		Paris	
AUGUST	Return to U.S.A.	New York	
SEPTEMBER			*Africa and Human Origins (The Appearance of Man)*
1955 JANUARY			*Barrière de la mort*
MARCH			*Le Christique*
10 APRIL	Dies on Easter Day		*Recherche, travail et adoration*

Works of Teilhard de Chardin

(Page numbers refer to quotations in the present volume.)

L'activation de l'énergie, Paris, Seuil, 1963; p. 191.

The Appearance of Man, London, Collins; New York, Harper, 1965, pp. 63, 91, 202.

The Future of Man, London, Collins,; New York, Harper, 1964, pp. 159, 171, 178.

Écrits du temps de la guerre, Paris, Grasset, 1965, pp. 16, 37, 44, 58.

L'énergie humaine, Paris, Seuil, 1962, pp. 98, 136, 138, 140, 144.

The Making of a Mind, London, Collins; New York, Harper, 1965, pp. 52, 53.

Hymn of the Universe, London, Collins; New York, Harper, 1965, pp. 53, 60, 72.

Letters from Egypt, New York, Herder & Herder, 1965, pp. 33, 34, 35.

Lettres d'Hastings et de Paris, Paris, Aubier, 1966, pp. 39, 42, 47-9.

Lettres à Léontine Zanta, Paris, Desclée de Brouwer, 1965, pp. 71-2, 78-9.

Letters from a Traveller, London, Collins; New York, Harper, 1962, pp. 68, 70-1, 74, 77, 83, 88, 92, 100, 104, 117, 121, 123, 127, 128, 131, 135, 140-6, 153, 158, 162, 165, 167, 168, 178, 184, 186, 189, 199.

Le Milieu Divin, (in translation), London, Collins; *The Divine Milieu*, New York, Harper, 1960, pp. 128, 176, 213.

The Phenomenon of Man, London, Collins; New York, Harper, 1959, p. 133.

Science et Christ, Paris, Seuil, 1965, p. 186.

The Vision of the Past, London, Collins; New York, Harper, 1966, pp. 90, 127.

OTHER WORKS REFERRED TO IN THE ALBUM

AUDOUIN-DUBREUIL, LOUIS, *Sur la route de la soie*, Paris, Plon, 1935, p. 115.

BARBOUR, GEORGE B., *With Teilhard de Chardin in the Field*, New York, Herder & Herder, 1965, pp. 181-2.

BREMOND, HENRI, *Le charme d'Athènes*, Paris, Bloud et Gay, 1953, p. 18.

CUÉNOT, CLAUDE, *Teilhard de Chardin: A Biographical Study*, London, Burns & Oates; Baltimore, Helicon Press; 1965, pp. 35, 64, 101, 158, 176, 186, 188, 190, 194, 197, 200.

LE FÈVRE, GEORGES, *La croisière jaune*, Paris, Plon, 1933, pp. 101-3, 107-8, 111-13.

TEILHARD DE CHARDIN, M-M, *L'énergie spirituelle de la souffrance*, Paris, Seuil, 1951, p. 136.

DE TERRA, HELMUT, *Memories of Teilhard de Chardin*, London, Collins; New York, Harper, 1964, pp. 148-9, 155.

Note: French titles refer to works and writings not yet translated into English.

The preface to this book by André George was first published in *Le Figaro* on 8th April, 1965.

Illustrations

Coll. Mme Victor Teilhard de Chardin: p. 7, 10, 11 a and b, 13, 17 (photo P. Gendraud, Clermont-Ferrand), 18, 21, 24 (photo M. A. Héraud, Aix-en-Provence), 28 a (photo Lefièvre-Couton, Clermont), 42 (photo Léon Caron, Amiens), 43, 57, 118, 136. — Coll. M. Joseph Teilhard de Chardin: p. 6, 8 (photo Pierson et Braun), 9 a (photo Pierson et Braun), 28 b (photo Lefièvre-Couton), 182 a and b. — Coll. M. Régis Teilhard de Chardin: p. 9 b, 12 a. — Coll. Mlle Alice Teillard-Chambon: p. 12 b (photo P. Gendraud), 14 (photo P. Gendraud), 15 (photo P. Gendraud), 52 a, 55, 56, 65 (photo Lefièvre-Couton), 77, 79 a and b, 126 (photo G. L. Manuel), 142 (*New York Herald Tribune*, 1937), 195. Archives de la Fondation Teilhard de Chardin: p. 26, 27, 35 a, 38, 70, 71 a, 73, 74, 75 b, 86-87, 88, 89, 90, 91, 92, 96 a, 97 r and l, 102, 105 b, 109, 111, 114, 115, 116, 124, 125, 132, 134, 135, 140 b, 148 b, 149 b, 152, 162 a and b, 163, 167, 168 a and b, 169, 171 a and b, 186, 187, 188, 189, 190 b, 191, 193, 194, 197, 198, 200 b, 201, 202, 205, 206. Archives Académie des Sciences: p. 84 — American Museum of Natural History, New York: p. 160-161, 204, 207, 208-209. — Photo Apkar, Alexandria: p. 34 b. — Archives de la Province S. J. de Lyon: p. 19, 33. — Archives de la Province S. J. de Paris: p. 30, 44 (photo Levenq et Cottin, Lyon). — Associated Press: p. 142 a. — Coll. George Barbour: p. 119, 120, 123. — Photos Max-H. Bégouën: p. 78, 158, 159 a and b. — Bibliothèque du Museum d'Histoire Naturelle, Paris: p. 46. — Coll. R. P. Boné: 190 a. — Photos W. Bosshard: p. 138, 145. — Coll. Mme Marcellin Boule: p. 47 a. — Photo Cartier-Bresson, Magnum: p. 166. — *Chine-Ceylan-Madagascar*, 1937: p. 75 a, 100. — Photos Yvonne Chevalier: p. 176, 177, 179, 180, 183. — Photo La Cigogne, Lyon: p. 16 b. — Coll. J. D. Clark (Rhodes-Livingstone Museum): p. 203. — Private Collection: p. 172, 173, 174, 175. — Photo R. P. Cordonnier, Saint-Omer: p. 215. — Photos Dr Delastre: p. 103, 104. — Citroën Expedition to Central Asia: p. 105 a (photo Specht), 106 (photo Remillier), 108 (photo Morizet), 110. — Coll. P. G. Fothergill, University of Newcastle-upon-Tyne: p. 39. — Coll. Paul Fejos: p. 192. — Coll. Frères de Ploërmel: p. 26. — Photo Chanoine Gaudefroy: p. 99. — Photo L. and M. Gayton, East Grinstead, Sussex: p. 40. — Photo G.P.A., Paris: p. 32. — Coll. Dr Grunberg: p. 52 b, 54. — Photo E. Guiton: p. 31. — Photos Halsman, New York: p. 211, 212. — Coll. Dora Hood (University of Toronto Press): p. 121, 165. — *L'Illustration:* p. 98. — Archives Institut de France: p. 67, 68. — Photo Keystone: p. 53. — Photos Von Koenigswald: p. 150, 156. — Photos Pierre Lamare: p. 62, 63, 64, 81, 82, 83, 85 a and b. — Photos Lavocat: p. 198, 199. — Photo R. P. Leroy: p. 164. — Coll. R. P. Lourron: p. 25. — Photo Mme de Mallevoüe: p. 95. — Coll. R. S. Mason: p. 200 a. — Photo Henri de Monfreid: p. 80. — *National Geographic Society*, Photos M. O. Williams: p. 101, 107 b, 112, 113. — Coll. Nels C. Nelson, American Museum, New York: p. 48, 49. — *The New Conquest of Central Asia*, by Chapman Andrews, American Museum of Natural History, New York: p. 92 a. — Photos John S. Nichols, New York: p. 141, 143. — Procure des Missions C. M., Lille: p. 76, 96 b (photo Watine), 140 a. — Publicité R. Bardet: p. 35 b, 47 b, 71 b, 76 b. — Photos Quatrième région aérienne, Aix-en-Provence: p. 20, 23. — Photo Rapho: p. 94. — Photo C. Rey: p. 29. — Photos Roger-Viollet: p. 16 a, 37, 50-51 (Boyer), 127, 170, 181. — Coll. Marie Rougier: p. 22. — Photo Senett and Spears, Jersey: p. 61. — Photos Helmut de Terra: p. 128 a and b, 129, 130, 131 a and b, 133, 146, 147, 148 a, 149 a, 151 a and b, 153 a and b, 154, 155, 157, 158. — Photos Delia Tyrwhitt: p. 137, 139. — Photo Agnès Varda: p. 122. — Coll. Mme Vaufrey: p. 45, 92 b, 93. — Coll. Georges Zayed: p. 34 a (photo Apkar, Alexandria).

Maps by Yvonne Rebeyrol. Those for India, Java and Burma were based on sketches by Helmut de Terra. (a = above, b = below.)